D1439215

Liturgy and Learning Through the Life Cycle

LITURGY
AND LEARNING
THROUGH
THE LIFE CYCLE

John H. Westerhoff, III
AND
William H. Willimon

The Seabury Press · New York

1980 · The Seabury Press
815 Second Avenue
New York, N.Y. 10017

Library of Congress Cataloging in Publication Data
Westerhoff, John H
  Liturgy and learning through the life cycle.
  1. Liturgics.   2. Liturgics—Study and teaching.
I. Willimon, William H., joint author.   II. Title.
BV176.W47   264   80-18592
ISBN 0-8164-0471-2

Contents

Liturgy and Learning
Through the Life Cycle

Introduction

This is a book for pastors, religious educators, members of liturgy and religious education committees, and others who are interested in the renewal of the liturgy through religious education or catechesis and the renewal of individual and corporate life through worship. It is written by a pastor and former pastor, who are, at present, teachers of worship and education in a seminary. We are both active in liturgical and catechetical renewal in our respective denominations—Episcopal and United Methodist.

This book arises out of our earlier work. In our previous books we laid the theoretical groundwork for a view of the church which places the liturgy at the center of its life. In those books, we stated the presuppositions and the reasons for viewing worship as the central task of Christians inside and outside the church. The liturgical life of the church, we argued, is directly related to the proclamation and enactment of Christian faith, Christian formation and transformation, and the pastoral care and cure of souls.

For instance, *Will Our Children Have Faith?* attempted to raise some fundamental questions about how persons come to and mature in Christian faith and, by implication, why so many of us do not seem to be fully converted or nurtured in that faith. That book noted that the church's liturgy is the principal setting for sustaining and transmitting the faith from generation to generation.

Learning Through Liturgy was a more explicit attempt to investigate further how people are shaped by and learn through their liturgical life in a faith community. In a chapter entitled "Liturgy and Catechesis: A Christian Marriage," it was noted that:

1

> Liturgy and learning have been linked since the birth of the
> Christian era, but of late they have become estranged. . . .
> gone their separate ways and attempts to reunite their various
> concerns have tended to confuse the issue and distort impor-
> tant distinctions between them.[1]

While *Learning Through Liturgy* was concerned to link liturgy and
learning, nevertheless there was a warning that we did not intend
to say that the worship of God was a mere pedagogical tool to educate people:

> Some religious educators have made the serious mistake of
> speaking of teaching *by* or *with* the liturgy, thereby reducing
> the liturgy to a didactic art. To *use* the liturgy is to do it vio-
> lence. Of course, we learn through the liturgy . . .

> Our rituals shape and form us in fundamental ways. But our
> liturgies should be understood properly as ends and not as
> means.[2]

In other words, while we are worshipping God, we are also expressing and experiencing what it means to be the People of God. Even
though the purpose of worship is the praise and adoration of God
and nothing else, while we are praising and adoring God in our rituals, we are also learning through our rituals. Catechesis, therefore,
is related to liturgics in two fundamental ways: through catechesis
or religious education, we need to prepare people for more meaningful participation in worship. Also, by examining what our rituals do to us while we are worshipping, religious education can help
us to evaluate and reshape our rituals where necessary.

Worship As Pastoral Care was an attempt to forge a link between
pastoral care and worship even as *Learning Through Liturgy* had
linked religious education and worship. One of the goals of *Worship As Pastoral Care* was to:

> . . . integrate the role of priest and pastor and to see some of
> the many ways in which worship and pastoral care can in-
> form, challenge, enrich and support each other.[3]

While admitting, once again, that the purpose, the goal of worship is the praise and adoration of God, this book also pointed out that "The pastoral care that occurs as we are meeting and are being met by God in worship is a significant by-product that we have too often overlooked."[4] Pastors were urged to use the disciplines of pastoral psychology to evaluate the adequacy and the human meaning of our accustomed worship rituals.

Word, Water, Wine and Bread was an attempt to bring together, in a readable, introductory way, some of the recent conclusions about the history of Christian worship, particularly in regard to the Eucharist and Baptism. This liturgical history was presented in order to,

> . . . recall where we have been in Christian worship so that we might see better where we ought to be going.[5]

The interest in that book was more than a mere antiquarian reconstruction of our liturgical past. The purpose of *Word, Water, Wine and Bread* was to give pastors and Christian educators the basic historical information they needed to make informed decisions about the future of our worship life. As was noted in the introduction to the book:

> Modern liturgical experimentation has often found that the path to meaningful liturgy requires us to journey again where the church has been before in order that we might arrive where we would like to be today.[6]

But it is one thing to argue for a link between liturgy and learning and it is another thing to forge that link in the daily pastoral leadership of Christian worship and education. It is one thing to see worship as a primary resource for pastoral care and it is another thing to care for a specific congregation in worship. It is one thing to know where we have been in the history of worship and where we ought to be headed in the future but it is another thing to actually set one's feet on the path toward the future.

We have observed, in our workshops on worship and in our visits to various congregations, that many pastors and religious educators know the "facts" of liturgical renewal and are in general agreement as to necessary reforms. But they have difficulty achieving in practice what they agree to in principle. In other words, it seemed to us that what is needed is a kind of manual, a guidebook through the church's worship for laity and clergy which not only describes where we ought to be going but *how* to get there. This book attempts to be that guide for the complete life cycle of persons and the church. An awareness of human development from birth to death has provided us with a new conception of learning and liturgy throughout our entire life cycle. Each of us grows and develops through the influence of internal psychological processes and external cultural processes. Human life is a journey or pilgrimage, but we do not plass through its various seasons without aid. Neither do we mature without assistance. Historically and cross-culturally, religious communities have provided experiences of learning and liturgy for such occasions in the lives of both the community and its people. Today the richness of this tradition is being reestablished. What seems to be needed is an aid for meaningful use.

For some, we fear, this book will be elementary, for others not easily comprehensible. It would have been easier for authors from one denomination to write this book for persons of their tradition. But while aware of all the hazards, we felt that it was important to write an ecumenical book. The whole Christian church is within a liturgical and catechetical reformation. Parishes in every tradition are at a somewhat different place; we often use a different vocabulary. Nevertheless, we need to learn from each other. Our hope is that this book will stimulate persons from various traditions to share and grow together.

Of course, it would be impossible to even suggest what might be done in every individual church to link learning and liturgy. Only you know your church—its tradition, needs, personality. Therefore only you can judge the appropriateness of what we suggest here. We also assume that we can only indicate general directions for your journey, perhaps suggest a few specific ways to get there, but it remains for you, in your own church, to draw the exact map and to do the traveling. Consider this book an invitation to the journey.

How This Book Is Organized

We have organized our thoughts and suggestions by first discussing the two major sacraments, the Eucharist and Baptism. We discuss these acts of worship first, and in greater detail, because they are the major initiating and sustaining liturgical events of the church as well as the norm and pattern for all other liturgical acts. Included in this section will be worship as it relates to the church year, the church's rites of first communion and confirmation as well as suggestions of a new rite for adolescence. Further we will touch upon the spiritual life and daily community and individual prayer. Then we discuss the pastoral offices of the church, the traditional pastoral offices as well as suggested rites of our own: Marriage, Recognition of Divorce, Thanksgiving for the Birth or Adoption of a Child, Moving and New Homes, Ordination and the Celebration of a New Ministry, Retirement, Reconciliation of a Penitent, Ministry to the Sick, Ministry to the Dying and Burial of the Dead.

Whether you regard these acts as essential to the life of your church, whether you call these rites by these names or other names we expect that you perform them, or something very much like them, in your church. For instance, no Southern Baptist we know celebrates the rite of Confirmation. But nearly every Southern Baptist we know worries as much as any of the rest of us about maturity in Christ and how the church can help Christians achieve that maturity. Effective Southern Baptist churches, even though they may not practice Confirmation as such, still have a complex of educational and liturgical activities which have the pastoral goal of helping people to mature into Christ. Likewise, no United Methodist whom we know uses Last Rites for the Dying. But nearly every United Methodist pastor whom we know is concerned and active at the time of death and usually follows a definite pattern of liturgical and pastoral activities to prepare people for death.

Our goal is not to convince you that you ought to call these activities by the names which we apply to them or even that you do them as we suggest. We simply want to help you think through what your church is already doing in its education and preparation of people for worship in order that you might do better what you are probably already doing in your own way. One of the beautiful things which are happening in liturgical renewal is the fruitful borrowing from one another's liturgical traditions so that, by this ecumenical borrowing, we are mutually enriched.

Each of the following chapters is divided into three parts:

First, we discuss the history and theology of the specific liturgical act with a focus upon liturgical norms. Here we will attempt to report, in a concise way, the main agreements of liturgical historians and theologians in regard to a particular rite. We will state what the rite means, where it comes from, and where we think it ought to be going in the future. In speaking descriptively of where we ought to be going in the future, we will speak of the "norm" for the rite. We use the word "norm" in the sense in which Aidan Kavanaugh uses the word: The *normal* practice and point of view of the church. By saying what is the normal way for something to be interpreted and celebrated we do not deny that a sacrament or rite may have been celebrated in an "abnormal" way in many times and places in church history. We are speaking of the standard way in which a rite is to be interpreted and celebrated. Once you understand the norm for a rite, it is possible for you to depart from the norm in your church's celebration of the rite as long as you depart from the norm for good pastoral reasons and as long as you keep the standard clearly in mind.

For instance, if we claim that the norm for Sunday worship is a full eucharistic service of Word and Table this does not mean that it is impossible for Christians to worship on Sunday without celebrating Holy Communion. It simply means that a full service of Word and Table is the standard, normal way for Christian corporate worship. When we deviate from that standard, responsible pastors and Christian educators must exercise care and creativity in order to ensure that the standard will be honored and that the full experience of faith which that standard upholds is offered in some other way to the people. As one of our high school English teachers once said of the rules of composition and syntax, "The rules can be broken if you are breaking the rules for good reasons."

The second section of each chapter will focus on educational or catechetical norms. We envisage a church's worship and/or education committee using this section as a springboard for the planning of a congregational program of liturgical renewal. Here we will offer generalized ideas for how a congregation might work together to prepare people for meaningful participation in a given liturgical experience. By implication we will also be asking if we are teaching what we intend to teach as we conduct our various rites. In other words, you will find not only ways to help people worship but also suggestions on ways to change some of our accustomed practices so that they might become more congruent with theological and historical norms and more effective in the lives of those who participate in the rites.

Finally, we will suggest norms for rubrics or directions for the celebration of each rite. Rituals are symbolic actions. What we do provides a key to their understanding. Through our behaviors we learn. It is therefore essential both educationally and liturgically that we explore who does what, when, and for what purpose. This section is not only for pastors. All those who participate in the church's rites need to understand why they do what they do. We hope that, through this book, pastors, worship committees, and other adults will be encouraged to explore ways to involve the laity in worship. Lay involvement in the Sunday-to-Sunday leadership of a congregation's worship is a primary way of emphasizing the shared priesthood of all baptized Christians. Whatever extent the laity are involved in the leadership of corporate worship in your congregation, this section will be important for everyone to read and understand. Pastors will be unable to lead in the ways we speak of here without the understanding and encouragement of the laity. In fact, some worship committees, upon reading this section on the leadership of worship, may find that they have to give their pastor some gentle prodding. The ultimate purpose of this section in each chapter is to discuss how we can lead the liturgy in such a way that we *do* what we *mean* in order that people are invited, through our caring and visionary leadership, to participate in the church's liturgy in some meaningful ways.

An Invitation to Reformation

Worship is a multifaceted, multimedia, multimeaningful human activity. When we worship, many things are happening. As stated at the beginning, the most basic thing which happens in worship, the purpose of our gatherings as Christians, is the meeting and praise of God by the people of God. But while this meeting and praise is occurring, people are formed by their worship. We form our rites but they also form and reform us in fundamental ways.

At stake here is the question: *How are Christians best nurtured and converted?* No, even prior to that is the question: *How is the church formed and transformed so that individual Christians are shaped and re-shaped?* This is the purpose of Christian education or catechesis. And, if not the purpose of worship, it is certainly a significant and essential by-product. We are convinced that the principal biblical, historical place for that formation is in the week-in, week-out worship of the people of God, those chosen people who, in their worship, to paraphrase Martin Luther, "are always reformed and ever reforming." Through that reformation, we are, we believe, being formed into that sacred image which God has intended for each of us from creation. This book is an invitation to more lively participation in that reforming work of the God who makes all things new—even us.

The festival of our lord Jesus Christ
Duke University Divinity School, 1980.

·1·

Baptism: Christian Initiation

We begin the Jesus story with John the Baptist. This strange, prophetic "voice crying in the wilderness" is depicted as one who "prepares the way" for the long-awaited Messiah. John's message is simple: "Get washed in order to be ready for the Messiah." John's baptism is thus a human sign of repentence, cleansing, and preparation for the coming of God's Kingdom.

When Jesus submits to being baptized by John in the Jordan, a dramatic change occurs in this ritual bath: the spirit descends and a voice from heaven proclaims "this is my beloved son." In the baptism of Jesus, the familiar Jewish rite of purification is transformed from a sign of human repentance and preparedness to an event of God's revelation and presence. There is now nothing to get ready for—the Kingdom is here—present in Jesus, the Christ. The baptism of Jesus is sign and seal that the inauguration day of that new Kingdom has arrived.

But Matthew says it was not until his earthly ministry was completed that Jesus commanded his disciples to baptize. The work of establishing the Kingdom, proclaiming its meaning, and revealing its presence is not done until Jesus has called his disciples, preached his message, invited the poor and outcast to his Gospel feast, and submitted to death upon the cross. In fact, in moving toward that death, he speaks of his death as his "baptism." "I have a baptism to be baptized with; and how I am constrained until it is accomplished!" (Luke 12:50) It is only after that death, that final baptismal work of loving submission and its following sign of victory on

9

Easter morning that the Risen Christ then commands his disciples to begin their baptizing: "Go therefore and make disciples of all nations, baptizing them in the name of the Father and of the Son and of the Holy Spirit, teaching them to observe all that I have commanded you. . . ." (Matthew 28:19–20a)

Jesus came preaching not merely a new religious idea, a new social programme, or even a new life-style. He came to inaugurate a Kingdom and to invite men and women to membership in that Kingdom. He formed a community which would bear his proclamation, form his people, celebrate his victory, submit itself to his discipline, and see itself as his body on this earth. To these disciples who bore his promised gift of the Spirit, he gave his message and his mandate: Go make disciples, baptizing and teaching. Baptism is the initiating, converting act; teaching is the ongoing, sustaining, nurturing act by which disciples are made.

Baptism is that sacrament, that activity where, by "water and the word," the beginning of God's saving work in us is both signified and accomplished. That initiating work is more a lifelong process than a momentary rite, an activity which, to paraphrase Luther, is a once-and-for-all sacrament which takes your whole life to finish. Baptism signifies that Christians are made—not born; that radical, lifelong submission through repentance and conversion is required of all who heed the Gospel call. In addition, Baptism not only starts us on the way of faith, it also signifies, to the whole world, that we are among the company of those who are signed, sealed, owned, claimed, and commissioned by Christ to do his work in the world:

> Once you were no people but now you are God's people; once you had not received mercy but now you have received mercy.
>
> I Peter 2:10

While the New Testament says little about the specifics of *how* we are to baptize or the qualifications of *whom* we are to baptize, or *when* we are to baptize, the New Testament is replete with images for the *meaning* of baptism. In the New Testament, baptism means everything that water means: cleansing ("But you have been through the purifying waters;" I Cor. 6:11), birth (John 3:5, Titus 3:5), death and life ("We were buried therefore with him by baptism into death, so that as Christ was raised from the dead by the glory of the Father, we too might walk in newness of life;" Romans 6:4).

The cleansing, birth, refreshment, life and death which take place in the baptismal process are no mere individualized experience. We are not merely born into a new way of feeling, or thinking, or acting. We are born into a new family—the Family of God. In baptism we are delivered out of loneliness into community and communion. To be baptized is to be "in Christ." To be incorporated into Christ's death and resurrection means to be grafted into the Body of Christ, to be initiated into a faith which is essentially a way of living together.

We have no full account of Christian Initiation until the *Apostolic Tradition* of Hippolytus, written in Rome about A.D. 200. According to this early work, the normal candidates for baptism were adults, even though children of professing parents were accepted for baptism and were baptized before the adults. The *Apostolic Tradition* depicts Christian Initiation as a long process of conversion and nurture in which baptism is not so much a beginning as a final goal.

Those who sought admission into the church were carefully examined by the church's teachers. Sponsors encountered a long and arduous process of initiation. They would testify as to the receptivity of inquirers to the word of God. Ethical standards were high. Sometimes costly changes in one's life-style were demanded.

Whoever passed this rigorous "scrutiny" was now called a "catechumen" ("hearer"), one who is deemed worthy of hearing the teaching of the church. The catechumenate lasted for three years. During this long period of training, catechumens received regular instruction and prayed along with their teacher. They were permitted to attend the first part of Sunday worship with its scripture reading and sermon but were dismissed before the Eucharist since they had not been baptized.

When the three-year period of instruction and examination ended, candidates were given final scrutiny and, if their lives were judged to be ready for full participation in the life of the community, they were admitted to baptism. Baptism was celebrated after an all-night vigil before the dawn of Easter. As the first rays of light appeared, candidates removed their clothing in order that "nothing alien" might go into the water. Nothing of one's old life was to be carried over into the new. Children were the first to be baptized, followed by men and then by women.

Each person renounced "Satan, and thy servants, and all thy works," and was then anointed with the "oil of exorcism" as a sign that one entered the water only after a complete break with one's old allegiances.

The actual baptism was done by submerging the candidate three times, as the candidate responded to the three sections of the baptismal creed: "Do you believe in God the Father Almighty . . . ? Do you believe in Jesus Christ, His only Son our Lord . . . ? Do you believe in the Holy Spirit . . . ?"

"I believe" was the candidate's response to each question. When the candidates came out of the water, they were anointed with the "oil of thanksgiving," given new white robes ("Put on the garment of Christ.") and taken before the bishop who laid his hands upon them, prayed for them, and anointed them a third time, signing them with a cross on their foreheads and kissing them.

The end result of all this, the privilege to which it entitled the new Christian, was participation with the congregation in the Eucharist. After being blessed by the bishop, the newly baptized exchanged the "kiss of peace" with members of the congregation and then partook of the Eucharist for the first time.

But what do these ancient rites have to do with us? In this early pattern of initiation, we see a pattern which can be helpful in judging our present practices of Christian initiation. After examining both the biblical evidence on baptism and the process of initiation as described in the *Apostolic Tradition,* it is possible for us to speak of a *norm* for Christian initiation.

The norm, the standard for a full process of Christian initiation, involves three dimensions or requirements:

First and foremost, it is essential to have the presence and participation of the Christian community. As stated earlier, we are not incorporated into an idea, a set of good intentions, or a new feeling; baptism incorporates us into the dead and risen Christ and into the community which Christ has formed. Baptism is initiation. "Private" baptisms do not make sense, because if baptism is anything, it is a public, communal, corporate, family affair. Baptism sets the tone for the whole pilgrimage of a Christian by signifying, at the beginning, our dependency upon the community for our faith and nurture. The burden of baptismal work is upon the *church,* the baptizers; not the one who is being baptized. It is the church to whom the command to "make disciples" has been given.

This is why our old arguments over infant versus adult baptism are usually misplaced debates. The argument usually centers upon the proper age, belief, or attributes of the person who is to be baptized. In the Middle Ages some argued that a child must be baptized immediately in order to ensure that, if the child died, it would be saved. After the Reformation, some groups contended that baptism must be postponed until adulthood when candidates are old enough to "really know what it means." Both arguments tend to forget that the principal actor in baptism is not the recipient but rather the *church.* It is the church's belief, intention, disposition, and activity in baptism which is the essential actor (or, to put it more accurately, God working through the church)—not the person who is to receive baptism. As Peter told the crowd at Pentecost, we are baptized, not because of our belief, righteousness, or feelings but rather we are given the gift of baptism because "these promises are to you and your children." (Acts 2:39) The promises of salvation, conversion, growth, and life are *God's* promises administered through the *church*—not through the good intentions of the candidate.

Indeed, many feel that the main problem with Christian initiation today is not so much the state of our liturgies, or our candidates, or our education but rather the state of the average church. Too often we are in the embarrassing situation of baptizing people into a loose confederation of individuals who take no responsibility for the conversion and nurture of others, who do not act as if they really believe that the promises of baptism are true, and who lack confidence in their ability, by God's grace, to "make disciples." Baptism, in this context, appears meaningless since we are, in effect, initiating people into nothing.

This is why, while we may be free to initiate the children of Christian parents into the church (because of the covenant, future-oriented, graceful nature of the promises of baptism), we are not free to baptize children for whom there is no one to make promises or take responsibility. In such cases, we would do better to wait until such time as these children can respond for themselves or until the church can assume more responsibility for their nurture. Of course, the refusal or postponement of baptism in such cases is invariably a judgment on the inadequacies of the church rather than upon the inadequacies of the candidate.

The norm which requires the presence and the participation of a believing, witnessing, caring Christian community ever reminds us that a seriousness about Christian initiation requires a new seriousness about the church.

A second requirement for a full, normal rite of Christian initiation is the presence of a responding candidate. We are admitting that this implies that the candidate is a mature person, an adult. While it is clear that the children of baptized Christians were baptized by the church from very early times, the norm for Christian initiation is an adult catechumenate. From the description of initiation which we see in the *Apostolic Tradition* it is clear that baptism not only speaks of future promises and unmerited grace, baptism also involves present conversion, renunciation of one's past, repentance, change, and learning. The subjects for Christian initiation are those who know something of the cost of discipleship and are willing to pay the price. Mature, adult catechumens are thus the most likely candidates for the death and rebirth which baptism demands.

However, to say that the adult catechumenate is the norm is not to say that the baptism of infants and children of Christian parents is forbidden. In fact, we think it is likely, in many cases even desirable, that this practice will continue. It is unthinkable, in most Christian congregations, that children should be legalistically excluded from full participation in the life of faith. The helplessness and dependency of children as well as their sense of wonder and joyful participation in a family's meals make them proper candidates for full participation in the life and meals of the family of God. Did not Jesus himself speak of children as first-class citizens in God's Kingdom? Congregations who can sufficiently claim, convert, and nurture their children should baptize children. The real question surrounding Christian initiation is not: How old should a person be before he or she is baptized? The question is: How can we best claim, convert, and nurture people into the faith? We are merely recognizing the norm or standard by which the adequacy of our rites of initiation must be judged. The practice of the baptism of the infants of Christian parents probably represents a pastoral accommodation or pastoral deviation from the norm which originally was done for good pastoral reasons. But when we deviate from the norm today, responsible Christians need to know what is at stake in the norm and what conditions are necessary to ensure that our well-intentioned deviation from the norm does not result in a spurious practice which distorts the witness of the church and is detrimental to the nurture of individual Christians.

A third essential element of a full rite of Christian initiation is water. Immersion in "living water" is the mode which is mentioned by Hippolytus. While the amount of water in itself does not make a baptism, the amount of water used is of great consequence—particularly great consequence for our understanding of and participation in the rite. It could be argued that our baptismal theology declined as the amount of water used in baptism declined. While there is some symbolic significance to all three traditional modes of baptism (pouring, sprinkling, immersion), nothing less than complete immersion is capable of conveying the rich death-life symbolism which we saw in Paul's baptismal theology. While we expect that all three modes of baptism will continue to be used by the church, we think it is important to be honest and cognizant of the deep, primordial, symbolic richness of immersion as the normal way to go about baptism.

The church is nothing less than the gathering of people who "by water and the word" have been made members of the Body of Christ. Baptism *makes* Christians by making explicit the union of Christians with their Lord within the context of Christ's community.

We have begun this book with baptism, not only because baptism is Christian initiation, the door to the church and its sacraments, but also because baptism is the sign of how our salvation is accomplished. At whatever age the baptismal process begins, it is a visible sign that we are always dependent, needy children (so far as our deliverance is concerned) who, throughout our lives, must rely upon others to sustain and nurture us in the faith.

Baptism is the first sacrament. It is not simply a prerequisite for participation in other sacraments but a reminder that all Christian worship is communal activity through which our Lord gives himself to us through the ordinary stuff of life and in the love of ordinary people who have themselves been washed, reborn, refreshed, buried, and resurrected so that they may in turn claim others for life in the Kingdom. There is no higher or more urgent task to which the church is called than baptism. In this evangelistic and missional act of naming, claiming, converting, proclaiming, and delivering people as *God's* people—we see the beginning and end of the church's message, mission, and mandate: "Go into all the world and make disciples ... baptizing ... teaching. ..."

Baptismal Catechesis

Catechesis and liturgy are closely linked. Both are pastoral ministries for and by the Christian community. Liturgy refers to both the daily life and labors of a people and the rituals or repetitive symbolic actions of a people expressive of the community's myth. Each, of course, informs the other. Our symbolic behavior shapes and forms our beliefs, attitudes, and life-styles; our beliefs, attitudes, and life-styles are expressed in our rituals. Catechesis refers to the process by which persons are initiated into the Christian community's faith, revelation, and vocation; the process by which persons, throughout their lives, are continually transformed and formed by and in the community's living tradition. As such, catechesis leads to more meaningful and faithful liturgy in terms of both ritual and daily life. Catechesis prepares persons for conscious, active, and genuine participation in the community's rituals. Catechesis also aids persons to grow in the knowledge of God, to live in closer relationship to God and to act more faithfully with God in the world; in this way catechesis aids persons to understand, evaluate, and reform their rituals. Catechesis, further, flows from liturgy inasmuch as ritual and daily life lead us to desire to grow in faith and faithfulness. Meaningful liturgy calls for informed participants; faithful participation calls for deeper understanding. Liturgy and catechesis support each other.

In this book, "catechesis" is concerned with *those pastoral activities that aid persons to understand the liturgical requirements of the Christian life and to prepare for conscious, active, genuine participation in the church's liturgical life.* In this regard catechesis can make three distinct contributions:

First, catechesis can provide opportunities for persons to reflect upon and understand the nature of their rituals, and the beliefs, attitudes, and life-styles expressed by them. [In one section of each chapter this concern will be considered under the title "Catechesis and . . . ."]

Second, catechesis can provide for meaningful experiences of learning within the community's rituals when that is its stated intention, for example in the Service of the Word within the Eucharistic Rite, in the sermon within the Marriage Rite, and before the absolution within the Rite of Reconciliation. [This concern will be considered under the title "Catechesis Within. . . ."]

Third, catechesis can provide opportunities for persons to prepare

for meaningful participation in a particular community's rituals.
[This will be considered under the title "Catechesis for. . . ."]

The section on catechesis in each chapter will explore issues and
norms. Catechetical or "content" issues will be identified. Similarly,
guidelines for catechesis or the learning process will be given. These
guidelines or norms will be generalizations. It is expected that particular human situations will call for exceptions. Pastorally when
there is a conflict between a norm and a situation the church will
need to make a pastoral decision on a faithful response by applying
the principle of grace—liberating and reconciling love.

While in most chapters we will suggest a few specific examples
of good catechesis, in no case do we intend to provide concrete catechetical programs. Rather, we intend simply to identify issues and
provide guidelines for the development of catechesis. Meaningful
and relevant catechesis emerges out of the life of a people. Each
congregation is called to take the responsibility for planning, designing, and actualizing its own faithful liturgical catechesis.

Catechesis and Baptism

If baptism is once again to become the sole and central rite of
Christian initiation a number of catechetical issues will need to be
addressed. Many persons in the church assume that baptism is an
expected, private, "family affair" for babies by which salvation, understood solely in terms of forgiveness of sin and eternal life, is delivered by magic to individuals. Others believe that baptism is a
personal, individual acceptance of Jesus Christ as Lord and Savior
following a sudden, dramatic, emotional conversion experience of
adults and sometimes children and youth. Since almost no serious
baptismal catechesis has been conducted recently, a host of secular
folk customs have emerged. Only a massive intentional parish program of catechesis can reform and resurrect this essential and foundational sacrament. While it does not matter if these programs are
formal or informal, it does matter that particular issues are addressed both in terms of what people think and how they feel.[7]
These issues are multiple:

The normative nature of adult baptism to which exceptions can be permitted only for the children of the faithful; the theological significance of baptism as the means by which persons are made Christians; the communal, public nature of baptism as a rite to be celebrated within a person's or family's worshipping community; the fact that baptism grants full and complete membership in the church along with the right to full participation including Holy Communion; the essential nature of lengthy and serious participation; the importance of sponsors or in the case of children, godparents who are chosen by the congregation and prepared to provide pre- and post-baptismal catechesis and companionship in the journey of faith; the nonrepeatable nature of baptism; and the need for the continual renewal of our baptismal covenant and lifelong catechesis will each need to be addressed within a total parish program of baptismal catechesis.

In order that a significant program of baptismal catechesis might be ensured, we suggest a few guidelines.

A group of faithful adults must be chosen and educated to prepare persons for baptism. These adults need a sound historical and theological understanding of baptism and an understanding of the rite of baptism; a strong foundation in Bible, church history, theology and ethics; a maturity of faith and life; a personal spiritual discipline; and the ability to offer spiritual direction and counsel. A parish program to equip persons for this significant lay ministry is the first step in any relevant program.

A deliberate, systematic and sustained church program for all children, youth, and adults, including retreats, parish suppers, newsletters, formal classes, bulletin inserts, sermons, informal events and the like, will need to be developed. No single announcement or program is adequate; a major commitment over a period of years is necessary.

EXAMPLE:

A yearly all-church baptismal party might be held; perhaps one year on the Sunday after Epiphany (Jesus' Baptism) to celebrate our call to ministry; and the next on All Saints' Day to celebrate our call to perfection or fulfillment and so forth. Intergenerational activities, using the arts and/or a variety of learning options appropriate to different ages which could highlight various aspects of baptism and its meaning, might accompany these celebrations.

Catechesis Within Baptism

It is expected that the sermon or homily at every baptism be directed to the meaning and significance of baptism in the light of the lessons assigned for the day. The sermon or homily has always been understood as having a catechetical function in terms of both *kerygma* (proclamation for conversion) and *didache* (interpretation for nurture). At least on the five primary occasions when baptism is celebrated each year (Easter Vigil, All Saints' Day, Sunday after Epiphany, Pentecost, and the visit of a bishop) the sermon or homily might focus on baptismal illumination.

EXAMPLE:

At each baptism, a small four-page educational guide (bulletin insert) on the nature and meaning of baptism, the baptismal liturgy, the necessary reaffirmation of our baptismal covenant, and the implications of baptism for our life in the church and the world could be written by lay persons and distributed to the congregation. Some of these could be specifically written for children. Over time, a small book might be assembled from these pamphlets for use in baptismal catechesis.

Catechesis for Baptism

Two modes of baptismal catechesis must be developed: the first for adults preparing for baptism; and the second for parents of children to be baptized.

The preparation period for adult catechumens is a serious, lengthy, solemn responsibility of the Christian community. It is marked by three stages. The pre-catechumenal period is best understood as inquiry to enable persons to determine if they really desire to become Christians. It is a time during which those who have been attracted to the Christian community are guided to examine and test their motives in order that they may freely commit themselves to pursue a disciplined exploration of the implications of Christian living.

Entry into the catechumenate is celebrated by a public liturgical act during the Sunday Eucharist. At this time a sponsor, chosen by the church, presents the catechumen to the congregation and assumes the responsibility of accompanying the catechumen through the process of preparation. During this stage the catechumen is expected to attend worship regularly, to acquire a knowledge of salvation history as revealed in the Holy Scriptures of the Old and New Testaments, to grow in the spiritual life of prayer and devotion, and to practice a life of Christian service and social action in accordance with the Gospel. From the time of admission, a catechumen is regarded as a part of the Christian community. The length of preparation will vary according to the needs of the individual.

Stage three is the baptismal candidacy stage. For a number of weeks before baptism the candidate and the sponsor are involved in private disciplines of fasting, prayer, and the examination of conscience in order that the candidate will be spiritually and emotionally ready for baptism.

A fourth period follows the administration of baptism and is devoted to formal and informal activities that will assist the newly baptized to understand the meaning of the sacraments and to experience the fullness of corporate life in the church.

Adult baptismal catechesis suggests the following needs:

We need to understand the relationship of evangelization to catechesis so that we might develop inquiry programs led by lay persons in which the Gospel is proclaimed and faith shared with those unbaptized adults who because of life crisis, transitions, or other significant events in their lives are open to Christian faith.

We need to develop programs for individuals and/or groups who desire baptism so that after we enroll them as catechumens we can offer a meaningful, lengthy (normatively a year) program including regular attendance at worship, spiritual life retreats, Bible study, conscience examination, discernment, and Christian service or ministry with their sponsors.

Intensive Lenten period programs on Christian ministry should be developed to meet the particular needs of those catechumens who have made a commitment of faith and desire to enter the final phase of their baptismal catechesis.

Last, we need post-baptismal catechesis on the mystery of the sacraments, the religious experience of God and social service and action on behalf of God's kingdom.

In order to make the baptism of babies a legitimate rite, a number of catechetical issues must be faced.

Baptism is neither a necessity nor right of children. It is a gift, which can never be earned. Children are to be baptized only if at least one parent is a baptized practicing Christian willing to engage in a serious and lengthy preparation program. An educational program needs to be developed which will help parents realize the serious nature and necessary discipline of this act as well as the legitimate and real alternative of waiting for their children to make their own decision. Guidelines for making parish decisions on who will be baptized under what circumstances must be framed.

Correspondingly, catechesis for child baptism necessitates that godparents or sponsors who are practicing Christians, mature in faith and piety (not only family friends), are available and prepared for this responsibility.

Perhaps we might first celebrate a rite for the birth or adoption of children (see page 132 ff) and at that ceremony assign godparents to prepare parents for the baptism of their children some months later.

Preparation for baptism is not solely an event for a couple's first child; it is essential for every new addition. Similarly, catechesis for other children in the family should be developed to aid them to understand the meaning of their baptisms.

Minimally, a yearly event or series of events for all members of the parish, perhaps during Lent, is necessary if the congregation is to adequately assume responsibility for the children it baptizes.

Further, we need to equip sponsors for their responsibilities and through them develop a significant program for parents which includes regular attendance at the weekly liturgy, weekly meetings for prayer, fellowship, and discussion of the meaning of baptism, and for an exploration of the spiritual journey, the devotional life of prayer and Bible reading, and Christian life in the world. Only after these preparations will persons be able to renew their baptismal covenant at their child's baptism. Following the baptism, a program needs to be developed which focuses on the spiritual formation of children and the skills necessary if parents are to fulfill their vows.

EXAMPLE:

Each year a congregation might offer a retreat for parents of baptized preschool children. At this gathering child-rearing practices, family life activities, and family rituals could be discussed and parents could be helped to share their faith with their children and to develop family life that might enhance and enliven their faith and faithfulness.

Baptismal Rubrics

While adequate preparation of both the congregation and the baptismal candidates is essential, we are convinced that robust celebration of the rite of Christian initiation is the best way to recover the centrality of baptism for the Christian life.

The norm for baptism (which we stated at the first part of this chapter) suggests the following guidelines or rubrics for leaders and participants in the liturgy of baptism:

No one should be baptized apart from the church—except in cases of unusual emergency. The church is the administrator of baptism, and baptism makes little sense except as initiation into the church. Lay sponsors of baptismal candidates, preferably sponsors who have had a hand in the candidate's pre-baptismal instruction or who will assume primary responsibility for post-baptismal instruction, should present the candidates. When an infant is baptized, it is a good idea for some person other than the child's parents to testify to the suitability of the child for baptism. The new United

Methodist rites suggest that a number of laypeople be invited to join in the laying-on-of-hands as witness to the ministry of the laity. Also, people are invited to testify to the candidate about their own faith and experience of baptism. Some congregations involve children in the congregation by having them gather around the font, watch the baptism, and then sing a song of welcome to the candidate.

Hospital or home baptisms are sometimes requested by unbaptized persons who are unable, due to serious illness or infirmity, to attend a Sunday service. Such baptisms may be gladly celebrated as pastoral exceptions to the normal method of baptism. They must only be done in exceptional circumstances, and then never done with the attitude that this is a "private" baptism or an "emergency baptism" to clinically ensure that a person will be "saved" in case of death. There are no "private" baptisms in the church. Baptism is not some magical, personal cleansing which is designed to preserve one from damnation. Such ideas tend to raise more troublesome questions than they do pastoral assurances and are perversions of God's grace and distortions of baptism as Christian initiation. When hospital or home baptisms are done, they should be done with pastoral sensitivity and with the presence of as many representatives of the church as possible to signify the presence and participation of the entire community of faith.

Each congregation should search for ways to make visible the linking of one's individual covenant to the congregational covenant. At various times of the year, baptismal festivals can be celebrated in which, after baptism of new Christians, all members of the congregation are invited to join in a renewal of baptismal vows. This service of baptismal renewal shows how baptism is more a life-long process than a once-and-for-all event. Renewal of baptismal vows can be accompanied by the asperging of the congregation with water from the font or simply touching the forehead of each person who desires to renew his or her baptism and repeating the words "Remember your baptism and be thankful."

The Episcopal Book of Common Prayer (1979) wisely directs

that the seasonal baptismal festivals be celebrated by a congregation even if there are no candidates for baptism. Even if a congregation has no babies or other candidates, it should not be denied the opportunity to reflect upon the continuing significance of baptism for the entire pilgrimage of faith. During these periods of baptismal remembrance, flowers or candles may be placed around the font and lessons and prayers may be read there in order to visually focus the congregation's attention upon this "rock from whence you were hewn." *Easter,* the prime baptismal festival, is a time to recall baptism's linkage to death and resurrection. *Pentecost* provides an opportunity to stress baptism as the giving of the Holy Spirit to all. *The Sunday after Epiphany* focuses upon the baptism of Jesus and highlights baptism as our call and commission to share in the ministry of Christ. *All Saints* sees baptism as our entrance into and sharing in the Communion of Saints. Episcopalians also see the *visit of a bishop* as an opportunity for baptismal celebration and remembrance, noting baptism as the rite of initiation into the church.

It may be necessary for families to adjust the date of their child's baptism to meet the needs of the congregation since baptism is not a private family affair. It is a celebration of the whole family of God, the church.

While we must resist the notion of baptism as a private, individualized affair, we should acknowledge that baptism is also a deeply personal event. The candidate's Christian name may be given and should be used throughout the rite (never the surname or family name). Some candidates may wish to testify to their own faith at this moment or to thank members of the congregation for their support and guidance during the catechumenate. As said above, a lay sponsor might say something about the candidate's progress into the faith. Baptismal gifts could be presented to the candidate. A large candle ("You are the light of the world. Let your light shine....") and a new white gown ("Put on the garment of Christ.") are traditional baptismal gifts which are rich symbols of discipleship. When children or infants are baptized, the exceptional nature of this event should lead us to search for special ways to help the baptized child grow into the meaning of this important occasion. A record or tape recording of a child's baptism could be a meaningful way to remind the child of the vows which the parents made for him or her at baptism. The officiating pastor might write a baptismal letter to the child describing the day and its significance. The letter could be read at the baptism and then sealed and put away until the child is old enough to read the letter for him or herself. A child's baptismal day could be celebrated on the baptismal anniversary. Confirmation or commitment to Christian service should be seen, along with other baptismal festivals and baptismal renewal services, as special times for baptized children and youth to renew and remember their baptism and to continue to grow into its meaning for their lives.

After baptism there should be time for congregational welcome of the newly baptized Christian through the traditional "kiss of peace." A lay leader of the congregation might then assign the new member some specific job to do within the congregation. Then the newly baptized could offer the bread and wine for communion (which should follow immediately after baptism). At the conclusion of the service, a congregational dinner in honor of the newly baptized and their families would be a good way to make this a special and personal day for those who have been initiated.

Finally, all of the new baptismal rites call for abundant use of water and a robust attempt on the part of the celebrant to lift up the rich and multifaceted imagery of baptism. A church's baptismal font should not be hidden in a corner but rather placed in a prominent position as a visible reminder of our birth and life in the faith. We think it makes good sense to follow the ancient practice of placing fonts at the front door of the church in order to symbolize the font as the entrance into the Family of God. Larger fonts will be needed by most of us. But, even if a church's present font is small, a pastor can make sure that water is seen, heard, and felt during a baptism. A pitcher of water can be effusively poured into the font at the beginning of the rite. If a church's font is very small or only a silver bowl, we have seen large, crockery mixing bowls which make wonderful "fonts" for baptism. Do not be afraid of a little water. The candidate should be believably, visibly wet—even if the celebrant gets a little wet in the process. For too long many Christians outside of the Roman Catholic and Orthodox traditions have distrusted the symbolic power of the sacraments. We have celebrated the sacraments timidly, verbally, and dryly rather than boldly, visibly, and effusively. In so doing we have cheated our people of the power and grace of sacramental experiences. Baptism is a good place to begin to recover some of the sacramental richness and power we have for too long been avoiding.

Only through such careful, intentional, robust celebration of Christian initiation can we make the disciples whom the Gospel demands and the world so desperately needs.

·2·

The Eucharist: Christian Nurture

The goal of baptism, the privilege to which it entitles one, is participation in the Holy Eucharist (the Lord's Supper, Holy Communion). From the beginning of the church, Christians gathered on Sunday, "the Lord's Day," and ate a meal of great religious significance—"the Lord's Supper." Some may say that the early Christians were pushing things a bit far to speak of eating together as a religious occasion. But sometimes the things we do most naturally and most basically are the best indicators of who we are and who we are meant to be. Christianity is, in some ways, a surprisingly mundane, materialistic, everyday kind of faith. Christian worship, at its beginning, was a surprisingly mundane, material, domestic-like affair which took its central rites not from a temple altar but from the dinner table in a home.

That Christians came to view the dinner table as the locus for their worship is attributable to their Jewish roots. For the Jew, every meal is a religious occasion, a time to acknowledge daily dependence upon the grace and mercy of God and upon God's gifts of food and life. Our custom of blessing food with a prayer comes from the Jews. Every Jewish meal is a sacred event because God is thanked for the food. When God is thanked, the food is placed in a new light. Food is thereby seen as a divine gift, something which is to be eaten in gratitude and thanksgiving.

While there are many special meals in Judaism, one of the most important Jewish religious meals was the Passover meal. Matthew, Mark, and Luke identify the Last Supper with the Passover (Matt. 12:17, Mk. 14:12, Lk. 22:7, 15), and Paul speaks of Christ as "our

Passover" (I Corin. 5:7–8). The Passover is associated with the Exodus from Egypt. When the Passover is celebrated around a Jewish family's dinner table, the master of the Passover Seder (the order of worship which the family recites on that night) proclaims to the participants:

> We were Pharaoh's slaves in Egypt, and the Lord our God brought us forth from there with a mighty hand and an outstretched arm. And if the Holy One, blessed be he, had not brought our forefathers forth from Egypt, then we, our children, and our children's children would still be Pharaoh's slaves in Egypt.

In other words, the Passover Seder is a celebration of God's mighty act of deliverance in the Exodus—not as mere historical commemoration, but as an event which has continuing relevance for God's people:

> It was not only for our fathers that the Holy One, blessed be he, redeemed, but us as well did he redeem along with them. . . .
>
> He had brought us forth from slavery to freedom, from sorrow to joy, from mourning to holiday, from darkness to great light, and from bondage to redemption.

One of the prominent features of the Passover Seder is the identification by the host of the food which the family eats: "This is the bread of affliction which your fathers did eat when they came out of Egypt. . . ." In the biblical accounts of the Last Supper, Jesus makes no use of these specific Passover ceremonies. His blessing of the bread and cup is typical of blessings at other special meals in Judaism. But whether or not the Last Supper was a Passover meal, the actions of Jesus at the meal would have undoubtedly recalled the table ritual of the Passover. When Jesus took the bread and the wine, he gave a different interpretation to these familiar elements, an interpretation which was unique to his own message and ministry but which built upon earlier Passover emphases. "This is my body . . . This is my blood of the covenant which is poured out for many. Truly I say to you, I shall not drink again of the fruit of the vine until that day when I drink it new in the kingdom of God." His death initiates the new kingdom of God. After his work is accomplished on the cross, the Lord will feast with his faithful in the presence of God. The meal becomes a sign of the inauguration of the kingdom, a visible, tasted, touched symbol of God's work of deliverance.

Whether or not the Last Supper was a Passover meal, it is clear that certain Passover themes (freedom, deliverance, God's mighty work in behalf of Israel, remembrance of sacred history) would quite naturally have been associated with the final meal of Jesus and his disciples. But it is also clear that the Last Supper came to mean much more than an ordinary Passover meal.

The "Last Supper" was not really the last supper with Jesus. It was the beginning of a series of meals with the risen Christ. In the days following the crucifixion, Christ miraculously appeared to his disciples. Many of those appearances were accompanied by meals. At Emmaus (Lk. 24:13–35), the despondent disciples were surprised because, "When he was at table with them, their eyes were opened" and they saw the risen Christ in their very midst. At that fateful meal, when Jesus performed the familiar fourfold action at the table—the blessing of bread, the taking of bread, the taking of the cup, and the giving of the bread and cup—their eyes were opened. He was vividly made known to them "in the breaking of the bread." (v. 35)

These subsequent meals with Christ were not merely repetitions of the Passover meal. They were common meals in which the disciples undoubtedly recalled the many occasions when Jesus had broken bread with them. He now continued with them "in the breaking of bread and prayers." At a very early date, the disciples came to understand these common meals as a sign of Christ's continuing presence with them, a foretaste of the kingdom of God, and the means by which the risen Christ would support and nurture them while they awaited his return. "Do this in remembrance of me," he had said. "For as often as you eat this bread and drink the cup," Paul told the Corinthians, "you proclaim the Lord's death until he comes." This "Lord's Supper," as Paul calls it, became the central, Sunday activity of Christians, the visible, active sign of Christ's presence in the midst of his waiting people.

In the Lord's Supper, many facets of the Christian faith were given visible expression. In one sense, the Lord's Supper means everything that any meal of loving friends means—only this meal is eaten in the presence of the Risen Christ. "I am with you always," Christ said, "Where two or three of you are gathered together, there I am also." This meal is therefore a sign of unity and fellowship, "Because there is one loaf, and you all eat from that one loaf," Paul said, "you all become one in Christ." The meal is a symbol for the manner of life which Christ intended his followers to live. In the sharing, serving, and unity which we see in this meal, we see an example of the ministry of Christ as well as the ministry of Christ's followers. Jesus only did in the Last Supper that which he did in all the meals which he ate with his followers—he served others. When the disciples of Christ serve one another in this sacred meal, they repeat the table action of Christ as well as the action of his entire ministry—loving service to others. It should come as no surprise that one of the earliest designations of ministers in the church was "deacon"—meaning "butler" or "waiter." We serve the needs of one another even as Christ has served us. Christians only do at the table what they are expected to do in the world—loving service to others in the name of Christ.

When the early church ate its sacred meal, it undoubtedly remembered not only the Last Supper but all of the meals which Jesus shared with the twelve—the feeding of the five thousand, the supper at the home of Levi, the wedding at Cana, the Emmaus meal, the breakfast on the beach. At those meals Jesus had been criticized for eating and drinking with sinners. The church, as it ate its meals after the Resurrection, now proclaimed to the world that Christ continued to eat and drink with sinners, even if they were sinners who were also his disciples.

But the Lord's Supper was much more than a mere meal of recollection. In the fourfold table action in which bread was taken, blessed, broken, and given, the early church actualized the mystery of Christ's continuing presence in its life. In Christ's obedient life, death, and resurrection, communion with God had been restored and communion with one's brothers and sisters had been accomplished. This was more than mere historical memory—it was a present experience which, in the meal, became available for all Christ's followers in the present and in the future.

One of the earliest complete descriptions of the Lord's Supper is found in the *Apostolic Tradition* of Hippolytus (cited in the previous chapter). It gives a full picture of the early church's Sunday worship which can be a helpful model for judging the adequacy of our present celebrations.

Hippolytus calls the Lord's Supper the "Eucharistia." This designation means in Greek, "Thanksgiving" and probably comes from the Prayer of Thanksgiving, the "Eucharistic Prayer" which is at the heart of the table action. The celebration of the Eucharist occurs within Sunday worship, after a *Service of the Word.* During this opening Service of the Word, scripture is read, psalms are recited, prayers are offered, and a sermon is preached. All unbaptized persons are then dismissed. The faithful then share *the Peace,* an embrace which signifies the unity and peace of the church. The deacons then collect loaves of bread and the wine and present them to the bishop (*episkopos*) who presides at the table.

After the *offering,* there is an opening dialogue between bishop and congregation:

> The Lord be with you.
> *And with thy spirit.*
> Lift up your hearts.
> *We lift them up unto the Lord.*
> Let us give thanks unto the Lord.
> *It is meet and right.*

Then follows the *Prayer of Thanksgiving* for God's work in Christ. This has also been called the "Prayer of Consecration,"

Canon, or Eucharistic Prayer. The elders of the congregation stand beside the bishop and extend their hands over the offering as the bishop stands and prays:

> We give you thanks, O God, through your dear Child, Jesus Christ, whom you sent us in these last days to save us, redeem us and inform us of your plan. He is your Word, inseparable from you, through whom you created all things and whom, being well pleased with him, you sent from heaven to a virgin's womb. He was conceived and took flesh and was manifested as your Son, born of the Holy Spirit and of the virgin. And he, accomplishing your will and acquiring a holy people for you, stretched out his hands as he suffered to free from suffering those who trust you.

This is a very Jewish prayer in its tone and content. Like Jewish table prayers, it blesses food by thanking God. God is thanked for his work in creation and in deliverance of his people from death and the devil. Then the prayer summarizes the core of belief about Christ. This second section corresponds directly to the part of the Apostles' Creed which deals with Christ and is a kind of summary of Apostolic belief in prayer form. It is not only a prayer but also a creed which states, in simple, straightforward fashion, the basics of Christian belief. It is also a thanksgiving hymn which thanks God by publicly proclaiming the mighty deeds of God in behalf of God's people, a joyous hymn of praise, making known and recalling to the congregation what God has done.

How different is this early eucharistic prayer from many of the eucharistic prayers which we inherited from the Reformation. Those Reformation prayers usually lift up only a small part of Christ's work, namely, Christ's work on the cross. The tone in those prayers is one of somber remembrance of the passion of Christ rather than a joyful proclamation of the full saving work of God in Christ. The opening phrase, "We give you thanks, O God. . . ," sets the tone of this prayer—a tone of joyful triumph of a people who have seen the work of God in their midst and who now gather to celebrate and take part in that victory.

Hippolytus' eucharistic prayer continues with three sections which are unlike the familiar Jewish table blessings. The first section is an account of the institution of the supper in words which are a free rendition of Paul's account of the supper in I Corinthians.

> . . .taking bread, he gave thanks to you and said: Take, eat, this is my body broken for you. In the same way, taking the chalice, he said: This is my blood which is shed for you. When you do this, do it in memory of me.

These words, which became known as the *Institution,* focus the meaning of the meal on the action of Jesus himself—not only his action at the supper but his action on the cross.

Then the *Anamnesis* (Greek for "remembrance," or "Memorial") is prayed.

> Remembering then, his death and resurrection, we offer you this bread and cup, giving you thanks for judging us worthy to stand before you and serve you as priests.

Note that this "remembering" is no mere historical recollection of a past event. Rather, it is remembrance in the sense of "re-representation" or "re-enactment," a proclamation of the presently manifested power of something which happened in the past and has present relevance for today. In this remembering, we participate in the saving events of the past, our time becomes that time. We are there.

The third section of Hippolytus' prayer speaks of the work of the Holy Spirit.

> And we ask you to send your Holy Spirit on the offering of holy church. In gathering them together grant to those who share in your holy mysteries so to take part that they may be filled with the Holy Spirit for the strengthening of their faith in the truth.

This is called the *Epiclesis* or Invocation and asks for the gift of the Spirit upon the offering of bread and wine and upon all of the participants.

The prayer then concludes with a *Doxology* ("praise"),

So that we may praise you and glorify you through your
Child Jesus Christ, through whom be to you glory and honor
with the Holy Spirit in holy church now and throughout all
ages. Amen.

The final "amen" signifies the people's assent and participation in
all that has gone before.

The offering having been blessed, the faithful now commune,
eating the bread and wine, then departing into the world.

From this account of Eucharist at the time of Hippolytus, we get
a picture of the early church's Sunday celebrations. The vivid, joyful nature of the rite and the simple, straightforward movement of
the ritual contrast with our usually somber, doleful, cluttered liturgies of the Holy Communion which many of us inherited from the
Reformation. The Eucharistic Prayer of Hippolytus has become a
model for nearly all contemporary revisions of the Eucharist. It has
helped us to recover a bold, biblically based and theologically full
Eucharistic rite which is a joyful proclamation of the mighty works
of God in Christ rather than (as many of our accustomed rites) a
sad and penitential cataloguing of our human sinfulness. It reminds
us that the Eucharist is not so much what is said as it is what is
done—a visible, active witness to the work of God in Christ in the
past, present, and future.

Careful attention to the Eucharist is essential for the church since
the Eucharist is basic food for Christians. In our participation in
the Eucharist, we are both nourished and formed for discipleship.
We therefore must take care how we are nourishing disciples in
the Eucharist. Just as we were able to discern norms or standards
for Christian initiation, it is also possible to discern norms for
the Eucharist by which we can judge the adequacy of our present
celebration.

First, the biblical and historical data remind us that the Eucharist
is the normal Sunday worship activity of the church. Whenever
Christians gather for Sunday worship and fail to climax that worship with the celebration of Holy Communion, they have cheated
themselves of the full experience of Christian worship on the

"Lord's Day." The recovery of weekly, Sunday celebration of the Eucharist is a pressing need for many Protestant churches.

Second, the normal pattern for the celebration of the Eucharist is a full service of Word and Table which moves from the celebration and proclamation of the word to participation in the fourfold table action. A Sunday service of word *and* table is normative. The Service of the Word originally served to nurture the faithful in the memories of the faith. It was a time for reading, storytelling, preaching, evangelizing, edification, and proclamation. This first part of the service also served to instruct the catechumens who were preparing for their baptism. Scripture is central in this part of the service. Its form is ultimately derived from the synagogue service in which the exiled Jewish community survived on the strength of its memory of God's past mighty acts in their behalf. Likewise, in the Service of the Word, the Christian community survives on the strength of its memory of God's mighty acts. This is also the appropriate point in the service for preaching which sets today's needs and questions alongside the testimony and promises of our tradition, to (as Karl Barth once said of good preaching) read the Bible and today's newspaper side by side.

Only when we have proclaimed and remembered and have been judged and strengthened by that proclamation and remembrance, are we ready to move to the table. While the Service of the Table is also a time of memory and proclamation, it is most important as a time of *enactment.* We have heard the Word—now, at the table, we *do* the Word. The Peace is offered, along with our gifts of bread and wine. The Peace and the Offering become symbols of what Christians do in worship and in the world. Then we do the fourfold table action: taking, blessing, breaking, and giving. This action unites us with Jesus' own action in the Upper Room and in the other meals he ate with his disciples. After the blessing of the gifts in the Prayer of Thanksgiving or Eucharistic Prayer, God's people, having blessed the food by thinking of their past and thanking God for his mighty deeds, are now ready for Communion. We are fed.

It is possible to discern a basic historical pattern or structure for

the Eucharist. The various acts of worship can be formed in congruence with this basic pattern to devise an order of worship.
Below is a Sunday structure which parallels not only this historical
pattern but also the structure of the new services among most Protestants and Roman Catholics:

1. Gather in the Lord's Name (Call to Worship, Opening Scripture sentences, Opening Prayers, Greetings, Announcements,
   explanation of the service, confession/absolution here or later,
   etc.)
2. Proclaim the Word of God (songs, drama, dance, background
   information on the lessons, scripture, sermon, etc.)
3. Respond to the Word of God (Affirmation of Faith, sermon
   talk-backs, hymns, prayers, testimonies, dance, etc.)
4. Pray for the World and the Church (confession/absolution)
5. Exchange the Peace (greeting in the Name of the Lord)
6. Make Eucharist
   a. Take Bread
   b. Bless Bread and Cup
   c. Break Bread
   d. Give Bread and Cup
7. Go Forth in the Lord's Name

Third, the Eucharist is primarily corporate and communal worship. It is an occasion for community and communion, not a time
for a personal, private meeting with God. Too many of us have
been celebrating the Lord's Supper in the same misdirected way as
the Corinthians before us whom St. Paul rebuked. (I Corin. 11)
Our individualized wafers, individualized communion glasses in
many Protestant bodies, and individual, self-contained, self-centered
faith have transformed a communal meal, the "Supper of the Lord,"
into "Your Own Private Supper" (as Paul calls it, I Corin. 11:21).
This is the antithesis of what Christ instituted. There is a place for
private worship, but the Sunday Eucharist is *not* the place. Nothing
in the service should detract from its unifying, communal, body-
making function. As Paul told the divided Corinthians, "Because

there is one bread, we, who are many, are one body, for we all partake of the one bread." (I Corin. 10:17)

Fourth, related to the above norm, all baptized Christians are invited to the Lord's Table—all baptized Christians *of whatever age.* The practice of infant communion arose in correspondence with the rise of infant baptism. The church had the good sense to recognize that it would be utterly inconsistent to baptize children without communing children. Later the decline of the practice of infant communion in the Western Church coincided with the rise of misunderstandings of the meaning of the Eucharist. Today, we are recognizing again that there are no compelling, theological, historical, biblical, or, for that matter, human developmental or life cycle reasons for denying any baptized person—of whatever age—admission to the Lord's Table.

Fifth, the Eucharist reminds us that Christianity is a "materialistic" faith. The ordinary, familiar, basic stuff of everyday life—bread and wine—opens up new levels of communion with the divine in our midst. In communion, the Incarnation, the "embodiment" of Christ, is celebrated in a particularly vivid, participatory way. All of our senses are engaged in a multimedia, sensuous, multifaceted experience of divine-human encounter. We are required to do what we too often only think about. In the words of the Psalmist, we "taste and smell" how good is our God! As John Calvin once said of God and the Eucharist, "Remembering that we are creatures, God condescends to use the creaturely things of his creation to convey spiritual things to us." For too long, many of us have been in the grip of a passive, nonparticipatory, cerebral, purely rational understanding of the faith. The Eucharist can lead us back to a more participatory, more engaging experience of the divine.

Sixth, as should be apparent from our earlier discussion of the biblical and patristic roots of the Eucharist, the Lord's Supper has a victorious, redemptive focus rather than a somber, funereal, penitential focus. The early Christians celebrated their sacred meal on Sunday, the "Lord's Day," the day of the victorious resurrection—not on Maundy Thursday, the day of the passion before the crucifixion. The folk who gather around the Lord's Table are sinners, but they are *redeemed* sinners. With the possible exception of the traditional penitential seasons of the year (Lent and Advent), prayers of confession and other acts of penance should be seen as possible prior acts of preparation for communion—not as integral parts of the communion itself. For many of us who have inherited the heavily penitential, sin-obsessed, limitedly focused eucharistic liturgies of the late medieval church and the Reformation, communion is a time for groveling about on our knees and rehashing our catalogue of human sins rather than a time for standing up and rehearsing our victorious deliverance through Christ. Communion is the celebration of God's acts of redemption through our Redeemer by a people who know they are redeemed.

Finally, the Eucharist is an "apostolic" event. The goal of our communion, our fellowship, our proclamation and celebration of our redemption is neither mere warmhearted togetherness nor introspective inwardness. Our goal is to find ourselves offered, blessed, and broken at the Lord's Table so that, being fed and nourished, we may be strengthened and commissioned for life in the world. Communion is an evangelistic, missional activity which equips us for radical service and witness to the world outside the confines of our table fellowship.

"Go forth to serve God in all that you do," says the minister as he or she dismisses the communicants in the United Methodists' new *Alternate Text of the Lord's Supper: 1972.*

"We are sent in Christ's name," reply the people.

Word and Table belong together every Sunday. Without the action of the table, our Sunday worship becomes dull, verbal, individualistic, rational, and nonparticipatory. This is, unfortunately, exactly what has happened in too many Protestant churches who have cut themselves off from the Eucharist. On the other hand, without the Service of the Word, the Eucharist is in danger of becoming detached from everyday life and cast adrift from the central Christian story. This is what happened in the post-Reformation Roman Catholic Church. Fortunately for both Protestants and

Roman Catholics, we are again recovering the full, rich experience of Word and Table.

It should be apparent from the preceding discussion that the basic, normative shape or pattern of the Eucharist is quite simple. We are free to eliminate many of the accretions which have been added to our eucharistic services over the years—if elimination of these elements is helpful. When we get down to the basics of taking, blessing, breaking, and giving, eucharistic worship is really a very simple affair. However, we are not free to eliminate the bread and wine. Bread and wine convey, as do no other foodstuffs, the biblical, symbolic, and traditional meaning of the Lord's Supper. In order to nourish God's people, we must do everything possible to ensure that these basic symbols are lifted up and opened up for God's people.

Eucharistic Catechesis

Rituals serve three functions: they are the means by which community is formed and rejuvenated, the means by which order and meaning are reestablished in the lives of people within the community and the means by which a community sustains and transmits its understandings and ways to the next generation. These functions are aspects of enculturation and acculturation, or those processes by which culture is transmitted to one generation and adapted by another. Within the framework of enculturation and acculturation, religious socialization is a process consisting of those lifelong formal and informal means through which persons and communities sustain and transmit, adapt and transform their faith and life-styles. As such, religious socialization is a model for engaging in catechesis. Ritual—repetitive, symbolic actions expressive of the community's myth—is central to religious socialization, foundational to catechesis.

In one important sense we learn what we do. We act our way into new ways of thinking and feeling. We make believe so that we can believe. We make love in order to fall in love. That is why it can be said that we can understand people by observing their rituals. The Sunday liturgy of the church and in particular the actions persons perform during that ritual express and shape their perceptions, understandings, and ways of life. That explains why changes in our rituals are so difficult to achieve. It also explains why we sometimes need to reform our rituals radically and always need to understand our ritual life.

Catechesis and Eucharist

If our contemporary understanding of the Eucharist and the recommended changes in our liturgies are to be achieved, a number of catechetical issues will need to be addressed.

First is the normative nature of Word *and* Sacrament. For years many Protestant churches ignored regular Holy Communion, some Roman Catholic churches ignored sermons. A catechesis that will aid people to understand the essential unity of Word and Sacrament in the Sunday Eucharistic liturgy will be necessary.

The communal nature of the Eucharist also will need serious attention. For too long people have understood the Sunday liturgy as a private, individualized act. We have prayed by closing our eyes, kneeling, and folding our hands, a posture best characterized as "entering the womb." We have constructed our churches in ways that keep people apart in rows of pews and where the kiss of peace seems strange.

For many years the Sunday liturgy has been an event in which people tended to be passive; that is, they came, sat, listened, thought and prayed. Touch, smell, sight and the other senses as well as our affections and actions typically were ignored. Community participation and the use of all our senses and the expression of feelings must be learned.

The shifting emphasis from penitence to redemption as the focus of the liturgy is strange and unsettling to many. For years our liturgies have emphasized our fallen human condition through repetitious acknowledgment of our sinful state and repetitious pleas for divine forgiveness. These liturgies were somber and doleful. Now that the redemptive message of the Gospel is the focus of the liturgy again, a more festive and celebrative style is appropriate. To understand this paradox of the faith and engage meaningfully in a redemptive, joyful Eucharist will require an imaginative catechesis which takes seriously old biases and opens up new possibilities not only about the nature of the Eucharist but also about our human nature.

Another issue is the family character of the Eucharist. For too long children have been isolated from the adult liturgy. Some complained that children bothered their private meditation, and others claimed that children could not understand the intellectualized service adults thought appropriate. A rediscovery of the affections and the importance of the intuitive mode of consciousness in worship once again makes it possible for children and adults to participate together. There is general agreement that children ought to be included, but we are not sure or agreed on what this implies for worship. There is also a growing conviction that all baptized children should be accepted joyfully at the Holy Communion. However, the full meaningful participation of children in the liturgy may present the most difficult problem for catechesis to address.

Last is the apostolic nature of the Sunday liturgy. The purpose of the Eucharist is to stimulate and equip both individuals and the community for ministry and mission in the world. No longer can the liturgy be used as an escape from personal or social problems. Still, if this apostolic intention is to prevail catechesis is presented with a difficult challenge.

If any of our new Eucharistic liturgies are to be accepted, understood, and made relevant to people, we must make massive, deliberate, systematic and sustained efforts to educate children and youth and reeducate adults. Too few congregations have been prepared for these changes. Both clergy and laity are confused and troubled; they express their frustrations by either ignoring the new rituals and their rubrics or by not fully participating in them.

Beginning with liturgy or worship committees, official church boards, and congregational leaders, Eucharistic catechesis must find ways to help people understand the history and emphasize the theology of worship in the church. More important will be to restore the ignored relationship between worship and work. It will not be simple to help people either see or integrate liturgy and life—that is, to live the Eucharist.

Perhaps, for a time, it will be necessary to have liturgies for children in some congregations. Those who choose this route should do so only as a strategy to introduce the new liturgies; their aim should be the eventual participation of all together. Our contention, however, is that we begin with adult catechesis. Only if we transform the lives, beliefs, attitudes and behavior of adults will we be able to adequately nurture our children.

In any case, congregational catechetical programs during the next decade will need to focus on Baptism and the Eucharist. Unless we address these two sacraments adequately little else that we do will have lasting significance.

EXAMPLE:

During Eastertide at the seventh anniversary of a child's baptism/first communion, parents, having prepared during lent, could provide a series of group exercises for their children to help them understand the Eucharist.

Further, on a Sunday evening or week night the congregation could gather and experience the liturgy with explanation before and reflection after each aspect. Other appropriate learning experiences for young children could be offered during this educational Eucharist.

Catechesis Within the Eucharist

Earlier we noted the two main divisions in the Eucharist: the Service of the Word and the Service of the Table or the *missa catechumenorum* (the liturgy of the faithful). Corresponding to the synagogue service with its rabbi or teacher, the purpose of the liturgy of the word in the early church was catechetical. Indeed catechesis—the edification and illumination of the community's myth—was the dominant mode of the first half of a liturgy in which instruction and worship were intertwined. During the liturgy of the catechumens, the congregation heard the faith proclaimed, learned the community's story, had that story interpreted and its implications extolled through oral instruction. It is incumbent upon us to take seriously what we now know about learning today as we shape this part of the liturgy. Once again catechesis must become the dominant note in the Service of the Word.

If learning within our liturgy is to be taken seriously, we must reestablish storytelling, music, discussion, drama, dance, film, and the graphic arts to a place of prominence. Dull readings of lessons which ignore their context and their authors' intentions must stop. Many lessons are better communicated through narrative storytelling or dramatic reenactment in the form of drama or dance. Singing of various kinds can take the place of spoken words. Remembering that our actions are as important as our words, the total congregation can be incorporated into the drama of the liturgy and the reenactment of our story. Visual learning through film, costumes, banners, and decorations can be introduced. A sermon can assume many of the same characteristics as it seeks to integrate the story of Jesus Christ and our story and thereby illumine the lessons. The arts have always been a major source of illumination. If we begin to understand the place of catechesis in the Service of the Word, and if we begin to make greater use of the arts and congregational participation, children, youth, and adults will once again find it meaningful to worship together; further, catechesis will occur within the liturgy of the catechumens for us all.

Perhaps if we began to include children all this would come to pass. What we *don't need* are children's sermons with their inadequate theology and patronizing attitude toward children. Instead, we need sermons that speak to children and adults. We need festive childlike celebrations which enhance the receptive mode of consciousness in both adults and children. Once we do this, people will again be able to see the Kingdom of God and to experience the presence of God in their lives.

EXAMPLE:

A group of families could be responsible for the Service of the Word at services during a season or for a series of weeks. In the previous season or weeks, this group could gather for catechesis and planning. Over the years a significant number of persons would be prepared for more meaningful participation and leadership in worship.

Catechesis for Eucharist

One last point. We will recommend and defend later the idea that all baptized children should participate in the Eucharist, and that parents are responsible for their children's Eucharistic Catechesis. In order for this to be operative, the church must develop a program to help parents perform this important task.

Children who have been receiving communion since their baptism should be provided Eucharistic Catechesis during their childhood years. In the preschool years this is primarily the responsibility of parents. Parents can help their children understand that: Communion is a special meal, a thanksgiving party with Jesus; the church is a family which eats together and loves each other; love is being accepted—just as you are, for nothing; and just as food is for health and growth, communion nourishes us so we can work for a better world. One of the best ways for children to learn these lessons is through bedtime stories. Parents could be helped to write such stories for their children. In later childhood, parents, the congregation and the clergy need to join together to reflect on their experience of sharing in the Eucharist and to be introduced to the church's attempts to understand this divine mystery. An alternative, in some congregations, would be a more formal program for children in preparation for a communal rite of admission to their first communion.

In any case, eucharistic catechesis is not a one-time program but a lifelong event.

For too long we have estranged catechesis and liturgy. The challenge of the future is to find new ways to integrate them within parish life. Perhaps the best way to accomplish this aim is to connect catechesis with the preparation of all ages for the Sunday liturgy.

Our suggestion is that the church school classes, as well as other bodies, be used for this preparation. At the center of the weekly liturgy are assigned lessons from the Old Testament, the Psalms, the Epistles of Paul, and the Gospels. The church's lectionary, now agreed upon by Roman Catholics and most Protestant bodies, related to the seasons and celebration of the church's year, can become the focus of our weekly catechesis. In other words, the lectionary can become the curriculum resource of our Sunday church schools. Whether it is in formal, age-graded classes meeting weekly or informal, intergenerational groupings meeting occasionally does not matter. What is essential is that the congregation prepare for its weekly eucharistic feast by learning to know, interpret, live, and do the Word of God as contained in the lectionary texts.

At the center of the church's life is the biblical story. Whenever and wherever that story and our story come together, human life is transformed and formed by Christian faith. Perhaps, Christmas is such a significant event in the lives of people because the Christmas story has been learned, lived, and internalized better than any other aspect of the Christian story. We need to be able to experience similar learning around the whole Christian story every Sunday of the year.

Sunday worship is to be the focal point in our lives. The Scripture is at the heart of that liturgy. Children, youth, and adults should focus their catechesis on the biblical story if the liturgy is to enhance and enliven our faith and lives and if our catechesis is to be relevant to the Gospel. We cannot give people faith. Nor can we teach faith. But we can share the faith story as our story and thereby encourage the gift of faith. Sharing, experiencing, and living that story needs to become the first aim of a catechesis which prepares us for participation in the church's Sunday liturgy.

Parish catechesis can be transformed by understanding the purpose of church school as preparing the whole congregation for its liturgy, its ritual and its life in the world. There is no better form of fundamental adult catechesis than the study of Scripture and the development of ways to share that Scripture and its personal meanings with children. That is why it is also best if churches develop their own resources for catechesis, resources which are first and foremost bound in the lives of their adults who share their faith by being with children in preparation for worship, in worship, and in daily life.

The future of parish catechesis is with those congregations who develop their own unique and diverse means to unite liturgy and learning.

EXAMPLE:

Each year a series of sessions might be held for parents of children baptized during the year. At those sessions parents should be prepared to help their children understand the Eucharist.

Further, on the fifth (or sixth) anniversary of a child's baptism and first Communion, a short series of events might be held for children to share their understanding of the Eucharist, to celebrate their place in the family and at the family meal, and to grow in the understanding of Communion. At this time they might be given the opportunity to choose a saint whom they would like for a friend and whose life they would like to emulate. At the end of these sessions they could be given their saint's medal and have a special Eucharist for their families in which they assist. Such a program would be necessary if children were to participate in Communion from their baptism day on. It would also make possible an educational event to prepare those children who have not been participants at the Eucharist during their preschool years.

Eucharistic Rubrics

We noted earlier that Christian worship has a surprisingly mundane, familial, domestic quality about it. The Eucharist is not the place (if there is any place in *Christian* worship) for leadership by an autonomous, impersonal, robot of a priest whose leadership is carefully detached from the people. The leader of the Eucharist serves as host at the Lord's Table. Like any good host, the presider at the Eucharist should work to make people feel comfortable, welcomed, and intimately involved in the meal. The rigidity, formality, and impersonality which characterize many congregations' communions are a hindrance to the people's full participation in the Eucharist and a travesty of the meaning of the meal. As is the case in all other worship events, the leader of the Eucharist sets the tone for the assembly. He or she conveys—by his or her style, facial expression, and way of doing things—the general tone and interpretation which is to be given to the liturgy. Pastoral leadership is a crucial matter.

In churches that are not accustomed to celebrating the Eucharist every Sunday, the first order of business should be a concerted effort to recover more regular celebrations of the Eucharist. While we believe there are good biblical and theological arguments for more frequent celebration, we know that more frequent celebration is more a matter of pastoral and educational strategy than theological argumentation. People will agree to more frequent celebrations of the Lord's Supper only when they participate in celebrations which are helpful to them. The best way to "sell" the congregation on more frequent celebrations is to celebrate well. A pastor must plan and lead the eucharistic service in such a way as to make clear to all that he or she considers this service the high point of the church's worship, the summit toward which all else moves, the normal thing for Christians to be doing in their Sunday assemblies.

Unfortunately, that is the very opposite of what most Protestant pastors have been conveying when the Lord's Supper is celebrated. We have seen countless church bulletins which speak of the Eucharist as a "special service" which is offered in the church chapel early on Sunday morning before the "regular preaching service." This tells the congregation, in effect, the Eucharist is the "abnormal, special, unusual thing for Christians to do." Some pastors hope that, by at least having the Eucharist at an early morning hour, they may entice the congregation into more frequent celebrations during the traditional eleven o'clock hour. But it usually does not work that way. What usually happens is that, when more frequent celebrations are suggested, someone says, "But we have Communion at 8:30 in the chapel for everyone who likes that kind of thing."

Pastors should identify, as specifically as possible, why people resist the Eucharist. If they complain that it is "too long," pastors are free to adjust the service to keep it within a manageable time frame. Repetitious words and actions can be eliminated. When we get down to the basic eucharistic pattern, we are impressed with how few of our current acts of worship are essential. While the Eucharist should never be rushed or done in a kind of "cafeteria-style" eat-and-run attitude, the service can be adjusted so that it keeps within a congregation's time needs. Remember, the fourfold pattern (taking, blessing, breaking, giving) is all that is utterly essential in the Eucharist—everything else is secondary. If a congregation feels that its pastor considers the Eucharist to be a bothersome chore, or a time to forsake the preaching office and offer a little "homily" or "meditation," or an occasion for the use of foreign-sounding speech and archaic terminology, the congregation will be less than excited about the Eucharist. But if the pastor approaches the Eucharist with a sense of expectation, a quiet confidence in the rite's power to bless the people, few congregations will fail to respond. On Sundays when Communion has *not* been celebrated, when the congregation leaves with a sense that they have *missed* something, that they have been *cheated* of the *full experience of Christian worship,* then the pastor can be assured that he or she has succeeded in restoring the Eucharist to its rightful place in the congregation's worship.

A continuing problem with the Eucharist in many churches is the heavily penitential, somber, almost funereal way in which it is "celebrated." We hope that it is clear, from our opening historical and theological discussion of the Eucharist, that the Eucharist is a victory celebration for God's mighty work in Christ—not a sad funeral for a departed friend. Too many of our people still approach Communion as an intensely private, individualized affair—a kind of Sunday Rite of Penance. This distorts the Eucharist. The Eucharist is a communal, corporate, family affair. Fortunately, most of the new eucharistic services among Lutherans, Episcopalians, Presbyterians, Roman Catholics, and United Methodists stress this joyful, communal spirit. The careful introduction and sensitive use of these new services will help many congregations to recover the centrality of the Eucharist. Carefully selected eucharistic hymns can be the greatest help in setting the tone for the service. Congregational singing during the actual communion increases participation and helps to make this a joyous occasion. A hymn during the Offering can underscore the joyous, grateful nature of our gifts to God. Never forget, we Christians worship on *Sunday*—the day of Easter, Pentecost, the day of joyful triumph and victory—and our Sunday gatherings ought to show forth that joy and triumph.

The Eucharist provides an excellent context for a wide variety of symbols and symbolic activities which become the visible and active Word for the church. An opening procession with a lay person carrying the Bible is a fine way of symbolizing the Word as *our* Word, that repository of faith and practice under which we all stand. The Word of the Bible can also be highlighted by the use of one pulpit or lectern (as opposed to the so-called "divided chancel" arrangement with pulpit on one side and lectern on the other). The preached word is not to be separated from the read and affirmed word. Some may also wish to follow the old practice of a "Gospel Procession" in which, for the Gospel reading, the Bible and lights are brought out into the midst of the people.

The place for candles is wherever the Word is read—to "illumine" the reading and hearing of the Word—rather than on the Lord's Table. The Table is best left bare rather than cluttered with books, candles, and crosses so that, when the gifts of bread and wine are placed there, our focus will not be distracted by secondary elements. The Table ought to look like a real utilitarian, simple, freestanding table; not some heavily decorated, "religious" table or sideboard which is too stylized or decorative to be functional. Immediately before the Communion and just after the Offering, the Table should be set with care and drama, as the Holy Meal is prepared for a Holy People. This preparation increases the congregation's expectancy and underscores the Eucharist as a meal.

We must give more careful attention to the bread and wine in communion. As in baptism, for too long many of us have been nonchalant about the elements of our sacraments. We will not recover full, robust celebrations of the Eucharist until we celebrate with real bread and real wine. An amateur winemaker could be enlisted to provide eucharistic wine. Bread can be baked by families or other groups in the congregation and then offered with the gifts. This can be a good way to involve children in the Eucharist. The involvement of children is a pressing need within many congregations where, even though children are baptized, they are excluded from the Lord's table. This makes no theological or historical sense. Baptized children are fully in the family and should fully participate in all of the family's gatherings—including the family's gathering for the Eucharist.

Bread and wine should be presented in generous quantities in cups, pitchers, and on plates which are simple yet are of high artistic quality. The wine should be poured into one cup and the bread should be broken from one loaf in full view of the people. The breaking of the bread is a high moment in the Eucharist. The breaking should be done with the awesomeness and drama which are appropriate for this rich, symbolic act of worship. Never forget that "He was known to them in the *breaking* of bread." (Luke 24:35). This increases visual participation and sense of unity.

The elements should be given to the people in generous, gracious quantities. As the bread and wine are given to each person, that moment should be personal and intimate. The person's Christian name can be spoken, "John, the body of Christ, given for you." Eye contact should be established. The hands should touch. Congregations may wish to vary their methods of eating (serving each other, different postures for different seasons of the church year). The book *It's Your Own Mystery* (Washington: The Liturgical Conference, 1977) is the best guidebook we know of for leaders of the Eucharist.

Finally, as in all of the church's worship, we can do more to involve the laity in the leadership of the liturgy. It is the priest's or pastor's duty to preside in the liturgy and to lead the service. The priest should be responsible for the Thanksgiving Prayer as well as for the fourfold table action. But the laity may be invited to share in the leadership of all other aspects of the rite. Lay assistance in the distribution of the elements not only saves time but it is also a beautiful symbol of the shared priesthood of all believers by virtue of our common baptism. Laity can join the pastor (after proper education and reflection on the Eucharist) in designing and leading alternate Eucharistic liturgies. Laity should assist in Eucharistic leadership only after they have been carefully selected on the basis of their special leadership gifts and carefully trained for their leadership roles.

In so doing, the gifts of God become food and drink for the people of God. The hungry are fed and the Gospel promise is fulfilled.

· 3 ·

Community Growth in Identity:
The Church Year

When in the course of the congregation's year, there comes that Sunday morning when people make their way to church through falling, coloring leaves and a chill is in the air, and even though a bright morning autumn sun may be shining, people sense in their bones that winter is not far behind; when Mrs. Smith places her garden flowers next to the altar with the announcement that "these are the last flowers until spring"; and when crops are harvested, and early evening darkness and dry stalks and stems along the roadside speak to us in a melancholy way of the mortality of things—we know that the year is slipping to its close, the agricultural year and the church's year. It is autumn and it is almost Advent.

Most of our religious festivals had their origins in earlier agricultural celebrations. The roots of the Jewish Passover, for instance, can be traced to the festival of the barley harvest. It is not difficult to sense the agricultural parallels to such Christian seasons as Easter and Advent. In the myths of nature's continual, seemingly eternal dying and rising, primitive people made sense out of their experience of fall and spring time, sought to influence or at least to order their lives in congruence with nature's unceasing flow, and saw their participation in the rhythm of nature as a way of redeeming themselves from the vicissitudes of human life and the ravages of time. Enmeshing oneself in the perpetual rhythm of seedtime and harvest gives one the illusion of immortality. Fertility worship, linking our human aspirations to the eternal rise and fall and rise again of nature's passions, has had a universal, continuing appeal. In rural churches, where people still have an economic as well as an emotional, day-to-day relationship with nature and its seasons, the church year will naturally tend to be measured and given significance by a progression of seasonal festivals which are tied to agriculture. The liturgical year, with its origins in earlier agricultural festivals, will tend to make sense in such congregations in a way that it does not in more urbanized settings.

But even churches in urban or suburban areas mark their lives and find their identity within a rhythm of events which punctuate the year. These seasonal celebrations may mark the occurrence of such mundane events as the beginning of school in the fall, the opening game of the local high school's football season, the night before all the young families in the church depart for Christmas visits to their relatives, or the day when the local industry gives everyone a two weeks summer vacation. The dependable, predictable rhythm of special times gives a congregation its special identity, marks important transitional times in the lives of the people, and commemorates key events in the congregation's history.

Seasons and days are celebrated by churches for the same reasons that any family celebrates significant experiences in its life. Every family lives by a complex of seasonal rituals which the family celebrates with unvarying regularity in patterned, predictable ways. Each family has its own yearly rituals and recipes for the celebration of Thanksgiving and Christmas. Each family has its own weekly rituals: certain chores it does on Saturdays, certain prescribed (if unwritten and unstated) ways it begins and ends each week, each season, each year. This rhythm of commemoration and celebration is passed down in each generation. It is a principal means of forming the family and informing both outsiders and family members of who the family is. Unity, coherence, and identity are nurtured through the family's seasonal activities. "Our family always takes its vacation the first week of June when we all go to the beach," a young member of the family will tell an outsider who inquires into the family's identity. If one of these seasonal rituals should, for some extenuating circumstance, not be done properly, family members invariably experience feelings of dis-ease, disappointment, and disorientation—a violation not only of the meaning of the special occasion but of the family's identity. "Christmas just wasn't Christmas this year without Uncle Jason and his eggnog," someone will say.

The Family of God instinctively knows that in its yearly round of rituals, its identity is at stake. One of the reasons many churches tend to be conservative and conserving is that, like most families, Families of God feel that there is great value in "knowing who we are," in treating the family past as legacy, in dealing with time as more than the mere plodding, meaningless chronological progression of seasons. Our celebrations make time into "our" time. New pastors or new members of a congregation who unwittingly or insensitively disrupt the patterned rhythm of time and the prescribed manner of celebrating and marking time within a congregation will be quickly informed that "This is not the way we are accustomed to doing things around here." The congregation is simply protecting and nurturing who it is, or who it has been told by its forebears that it was, or who it dreams that it could be. In so doing, the congregation is continuing some of the church's most ancient dealings with time.

Keeping Time As Christians

From its earliest days, the church has claimed that a Christian's approach to time was not only important but also different from some widely held views of time. At an early date, the church adopted the Jewish practice of dividing the day into certain key hours for personal prayer. The "Hours" provided a system of daily devotions for Christians outside of the worshipping community. The days of the week were also assigned special significance, as the Jews had done. Each day called for particular kinds of prayer and devotional activity. We will discuss this daily and weekly prayer rhythm in the next chapter.

In the church's celebration of the Christian year we move through a pilgrimage of the life and teaching of Jesus Christ. Moving around the feasts of Christmas and Easter are the two major cycles of the Christian year: the Christmas cycle, which includes Advent, Christmas and Epiphany; and the Easter, or Paschal, cycle, which includes Lent, Easter, Pentecost, and the post-Pentecost season or ordinary time. In moving through the weekly or annual cycle, the church acts out who it is and what it believes about time. In fact, part of the distinctiveness of the church's identity is the church's distinctive view of time.

The Christian year may have some of its origins in certain agricultural observances but it is quite different from the view of time which is based upon the *fertility cycle of nature.* Professor Milton Crum has noted that twentieth-century pagans, with their myth of cyclic history and the eternal return of life, say, "There is *always* tomorrow." "There is *nothing new* under the sun." "There is *always* another chance." But the Christian Gospel says there will not *always* be the next anything, that history has an end point, that the time for decision is now, that our lives are more than victims of the ceaseless, purposeless grindings of the wheels of fate, that the risings and fallings of nature's passion are not enough to build a life upon, that the seeming eternality of nature is an illusion.

Not only does the Christian view of time reject the view of time which is expressed in the pagan nature cycles, but it also rejects a purely *historical view of time.* Israel gave significance to chronological time by interpreting the events of history as acts of God. History was more than the mere repetition of natural cycles, even more than a string of interesting but essentially meaningless and unrelated historical events. History was salvation history. The Old Testament shows that Israel experienced constant conflict between her view of history as the surprising, providential activity of God and her pagan neighbors' view of history as mere natural cycle. For Israel, history is redeemed, continuing testimony to God's dealings with us, a repository of our faith and a source of our identity.

The trouble with even so noble a view of time as salvation history is that it often results in our living either by past commemoration or in future anticipation. Our celebrations of time become either escapist nostalgia for the good old days, or escapist utopian dreams for the future. Past and future time consumes time now. Such thinking about time can be debilitating to individuals or groups, relieving us from the responsibility of living faithfully in the present, since our concern is either in reliving the past or in idle speculation of the future. The former danger is the inherent weakness in most revivalism—substituting the past for the present.

The church year—or liturgical year as we know it today—was begun in the fourth century. Under Constantine, the church made its peace with the world. No longer did the church see itself as a persecuted counterculture movement on the fringes of Roman society. It now saw itself as an integral part of society, a transformer or baptizer of culture rather than an enemy of culture.

Cyril, the fourth-century bishop of Jerusalem, developed a series of worship services for the thousands of pilgrims who gathered in Jerusalem for Easter. He led the pilgrims through a progression of services beginning on what was becoming known as "Palm Sunday," moving through a commemoration of the supper in the Upper Room, the crucifixion on Good Friday, and finally, a joyous Easter service at the site of the tomb. Holy Week was born. This practice of a series of commemorative services was copied elsewhere. Other special Christian days like Christmas or Epiphany were invented and added to an expanding church calendar and the result was the church year. The year thus became, in most Christians' eyes, a kind of liturgical clock, a chronological progression based upon some events in the life of Christ or the life of the church, which tick by year after year in orderly chronological progression.

But in its New Testament origins, the Christian view of time transcends and even negates the chronological, historical view of time. The Gospel says that we are in the "end time," the end of both the ceaseless round of nature cycles and of the ceaseless round of commemoration and anticipation of chronological time. Jesus came, died, and was raised to show the "eschaton," the end of time. The Christian view of time is best characterized as *es-chatological.* "Behold, *now* is the acceptable time; behold, now is the day of salvation." (II Corinthians 6:2, italics added) Faith is more than memory of past historical events, more than hope for the future; faith is present trust in a presently reigning Lord. Past, present, and future meet and have their meaning in that Lord. The Gospel is always the eschatological (literally, "last word") message to us that we have been freed for life in the present by God's loving work. The new age has dawned. We are now to live as those who already know the purpose of creation and how the last chapter of earthly history will end.

Sometimes churches tell the Gospel story as if it were a historical story. They see themselves as conserving, holding on to something precious, carefully guarding and passing on some valuable antique which has been bequeathed to them by past generations. But the Gospel cannot be reduced to historical observance. To do so is to destroy it. Christ is not some historical person who once lived and died and whom we now respectfully remember. He is a presently living Lord, a Lord who demands discipleship in the present, not relegation to the safe distance of the past.

The problem of Christ is not how we should remember him but how we should serve him. The problem of the Gospel is not the problem of the distance between Jesus' time and our time but the problem of the distance between who we are and who Jesus *is.* We often deceive ourselves into thinking that we have a historical problem, we treat the events of the Gospel as ancient history which must now be remembered and commemorated, we define faith as memory of the past rather than action in the present because it is easier for us this way. We can plead that we need more information, or that our time is too unlike Christ's time to be related, or that the purpose of our worship and preaching is mere recollection— thereby shielding ourselves from his present claims upon us. "Today is Pentecost," the preacher will announce, "and I would like to explain to you the origin and meaning of this day in the Christian Calendar." Such historical lectures used in place of Christian proclamation are sure to 'protect' us from intrusions of the Spirit into our tidy little museums of faith.

When the church year, or any of a church's rhythm of yearly, seasonal, monthly, weekly, or daily activities are used in a purely historical, commemorative, chronological way or (to return to an early point) a purely natural, cyclic way, that church's dealings with time are less than the Gospel's testimony about time.

We live "between the time"—and always have. Our lives remain stretched between the tension of the now and the not yet. In an age when millions submerge themselves in a new paganism which lives only by its passions, its nature worship, its astrology, its playboy fertility cults, by jogging and dieting its way to salvation and immortality, an important mission of the church is to challenge such pagan illusions about endless time. In a church where the past has consumed the present and the good old days seem more appropriate days for discipleship than present days, that church's pastor will need to proclaim a Gospel which sees the present as time for decision, action, and faith and which sees the future as time for hope, confidence, and judgment. We are in the last days—and always have been.

The church year can be a powerful means of communicating the eschatological, last word of the Gospel. The church year is not an optional liturgical device. It is a means of proclaiming the ever present Gospel not only through word (through the use of one of the new lectionaries, propers, and the observance of Saints' Days) but also through deed (in our relating of the clothing, art, symbolism, and order of worship to each season).

In its use of a special church calendar, the church is, in effect, obliterating secular views of time. It is saying that cyclic time is an illusion and chronological time is irrelevant. The present time has meaning only as the time of Christ and his Gospel. We move through the seasons of the church year, not to plod our way through a series of remembrances of historical events, but rather to proclaim the fullness of the Gospel in its many different facets.

Churches that fail to order their preaching and prayer along the lines of the traditional liturgical calendar and the lectionary invariably find it more difficult to give adequate treatment to Scripture and to express and enact the full Gospel in their worship. Much Protestant preaching and worship suffer from this paucity of themes.

Too many free church Protestants say they honor Scripture but then fail to read from significant portions of Scripture in worship. The Epistles are haphazardly read; the Old Testament is completely overlooked. Too often, when Scripture is read, it comes from the pastor's own favorite texts. The lectionary is a corrective to this neglect of Scripture. We inherited the lectionary (literally: "readings") from the synagogue where Scripture was read in a continuous yearly cycle. Until the Middle Ages, the church read three lessons—Old Testament, Epistle, Gospel—each Sunday. Sometimes the preacher would preach from one of these texts, although that was not the primary purpose of the readings. The primary purpose of the readings was the simple assertion that the People of God ought to hear the Word of God in their worship. During the Reformation, some people argued that the lectionary limited the congregation's free use of Scripture. But the actual experience of free churches which have failed to utilize the lectionary is decidedly to the contrary. When we have not used the lectionary, we have limited our exposure to Scripture rather than enriched it. The new three-year ecumenical lectionaries give us a wonderful opportunity to restore the Word of God to the people's worship of God.

Another major problem for many of us has been the ordering of our Sunday worship on the basis of denominational programs or secular festivals (Mother's Day, United Nations Day, Stewardship Sunday) rather than on the traditional festivals of the church year. This "programmatic year" can turn worship into a self-serving rally for the denomination's latest program rather than worship of God. We focus on whatever good works the congregation is being urged to do at the time rather than upon the good work of God in Jesus Christ for all time. The programmatic year cheats our people of hearing the full range of notes within the Gospel.

The church year helps to ensure that the great themes of the faith will be proclaimed, that the time we move in is a time of faith and hope, that the ordering of our life will be centered upon Christ and his continuing work rather than exclusively upon our works.

The church year, the lectionary, and the celebration of the saints are ways of enriching our worship, not by calling us back in time to past events in the Gospel but by calling us forward to faithfulness in our present living of the Gospel and judging the inadequacy of some of our current definitions of the Good News.

Most families already know the joy and edification which come from a yearly round of special seasons and days. The celebration (not "commemoration") of the church year is a natural way for a congregation to edify itself. But the pastor must take care that the time we celebrate is Christian, end of time, eschatological time. We suggest the following norms which will enable our celebration of the Christian year to be a time of growth in Christian identity.

We must be clear that we are not engaging, in our liturgical year, in a cyclic redoing of historical events in the life of Christ which are remembered in a merely historical way. Our church year celebrates the present reality of these events for us today. As we stated in the discussion of the Eucharist, the "remembrance" (*anamnesis*) of Christians is not historical recollection, rather it is remembering in the sense of remembering who we *are*. The church year gives us our identity in the present, not just our memory of the past. Is our worship a simply nostalgic or perhaps (in the other extreme) a rootlessly "relevant" endeavor which superficially repeats contemporary cultural values? Or is our worship an honest, painfully contemporary attempt to proclaim and enact the Gospel in the light of what we understand to be God's past and present dealings with us as well as God's future purposes for us?

Second, the church year is the normative way for Christians to order their weekly worship. The secular or "programmatic year," which has a way of moving from one denominational program to the next, is an inadequate way to order our worship life. The liturgical, christological year, enriched with the celebration of the lives of the saints, is the historically, theologically and biblically responsible means of ordering our time together.

Further, the systematic way of reading and preaching from Scripture which the use of the lectionary affords us is the best means for ordering our use of Scripture. For those of us who believe that the Bible is central to the Christian message and the Christian life, the use of the lectionary enables us to lift up the entire range of scriptural testimony.

Finally, Sunday is always the central act of Christian time. While the celebration of saints' days, special events, and the changing liturgical seasons can be helpful in providing a wide variety of themes and emphases for our worship, we must not clutter our calendar or obscure the fact that the central celebration, the central focus is upon Christ and Christ's work of redemption. Sunday is always "resurrection day," regardless of the season.

Cyclical Catechesis
It seems so obvious. The idea isn't new. Every family knows that its identity is framed and sustained by the moments, days, and occasions it celebrates. Every nation is dependent upon the days it sets aside for memory and vision. Individual and corporate life have meaning and purpose to the extent that those are days and seasons which act as occasions for telescoping and representing their understandings and ways. Our faith, our perception of reality, is determined by the days we name as holy. Revelation, our experience of the life in God in its fullness and completeness, is influenced by how we celebrate the seasons and cycles of our lives. Our sense of vocation and its resultant reflective actions are conditioned by the stories we remember and reenact. Only through the celebration of the past does the present take on character and the future have significance. Every feast and festival has both historical significance and contemporary relevance for persons and their communities. Advent not only recalls past and present expectations of Christ's coming, it also touches and symbolizes all our times of expectation and waiting. Feelings of anticipation are not limited to a season, but

by setting aside a special time to direct our attention to such experiences we make all such experiences holy.

The days we celebrate shape our lives. By experiencing and reflecting upon special moments, we discover the meaning of life itself. And through such discoveries our decisions and actions are molded and inspired. The church year provides us with a means by which we remember and celebrate the story of Jesus. Most important, it provides us with the means by which that story can become our story. Participation in the intersection of our lives and the church year can unveil to us the transforming and stimulating presence of Christ in our lives, and it can make it possible for our day-to-day activity to be informed by Christian faith.

As we share in the church's cycle of the soul, its festivals, feasts, and fasts, we each begin to discover our personal story as an integral aspect of the Christ story and the human story. The isolated individual self is a fiction. In truth, we are corporate selves who live in a continuous dynamic relationship with all other selves and with God. The self is constituted by its relationships; human life is essentially corporate. God created human beings with a need for community. We cannot be human alone. Community and corporate identity are not optional. We can only know who and whose we are, only understand the meaning and purpose of our lives as we celebrate time in the context of a community and its story.

Catechesis and the Christian Year

The Christian year, of course, has to be lived and experienced if it is to have reality; it cannot simply be observed by passive spectators. Every moment of time is an occasion for experiencing salvation. But without holidays our days will not become holy days. So it is that the Christian faith community has ordered the year in halves. The first made up of a Nativity cycle including Advent, Christmas, and Epiphany; and a Resurrection cycle including Lent, Easter, and Pentecost. In the light of the glories of these cycles, ordinary time is best described as second best.

Each year begins with the reenactment of human hopes and expectations. Advent celebrates our human longing for personal and social salvation. It is a season of visions and hopes, a time to recall our pregnancy with possibility, to experience again the eternal hopes for human life we bear, to share our visions of fulfillment and our need to wait with patience for the gift of wholeness. Christmas retells the story of God's coming to us in Jesus Christ. It is the season when we celebrate all moments of new births, new beginnings, new revelations of and insights into who and whose we really are. Epiphany recalls the movement of humanity to God. It is the season in which we celebrate our pilgrimage to fulfillment, perfection, wholeness, and health.

Lent relives Israel's and Jesus' forty days in the desert and in the wilderness, days of wandering, lostness, and temptation. It is the season in which we are reminded that we are born to die. It is a season to get in touch with the trials, temptations, and torments of life; a time in which we discover again our incompleteness, brokenness, poverty, and hunger; a time in which we make conscious our faithlessness and recount the ways in which we have deliberately neglected or denied God's will for us. As such, it is a time to remember our call to love God and our neighbor, to live the simple life of prayer and contemplation, of self-denial and corporate action in behalf of our neighbors' need. Easter recounts God's action to save us in the drama of Christ's resurrection. It is a season in which we celebrate our need to let go, give up control, and to die that we may have life more abundantly. It is a time to remember our need for rebirth and to discover again the hope and possibility of fulfillment. Pentecost retells the story of God's continuing presence with us through the Holy Spirit and the presence of the church to sustain us in our vision and empower us to lives of wholeness so that we might be a sign to the world of healthy individual and corporate life and that we might be witness to individual and corporate life in its completeness.

Through ordinary time we recall the life of Christ and thereby celebrate our lives with Christ. It is a season focused upon our mission and ministry in the world. Within the cycle of Sundays —feast days of our Lord Jesus Christ—each with its special significance, each with its particular emphasis on one aspect of Christ's life and our lives, there are holy days set aside for special observance and devotion. We have Ash Wednesday, Palm Sunday, Maundy Thursday, Good Friday, the confession of Peter, the conversion of St. Paul, the presentation of Jesus in the temple, the Annunciation, and the Transfiguration, All Saints Day and Holy Innocents and a host of saints' days. There are the biblical saints' days, such as Matthew, Joseph, Mary, St. Michael and All Angels. There are the saints of more recent historical time, such as Anthony, Chrysostom, Anselm, Julian of Norwich, Augustine, Francis, and Teresa. And there are modern saints, such as Camilo Torres, Luther, Wesley, Harriet Tubman, Bach, Bonhoeffer, Martin Luther King, Hammarskjöld, and Mother Teresa, each of whom reminds us of our calling and reveals to us one aspect of sanctified life with God and ministry in the world.

EXAMPLE:

A parish party could be held at the beginning of each season of the church year. Groups of families could plan and lead these events. For instance:

Advent: A longing for salvation or a celebration of our vision of God's kingdom could be held. A variety of art forms and scripture could be used with all ages to envision God's rule of political, social, economic justice and peace, unity and freedom, equality and well-being of all. At the close, our brokenness, incompleteness, injustice, alienation, and oppression could be acknowledged and our human longing be turned into an act of corporate repentance and a commitment be made to acts of penance that might be practiced to aid us in living for God's kingdom.

Christmas: A quiet time with God could be held in the midst of frantic partying and business of the season. It could be an event opening ourselves to friendship with God who comes in Jesus to be our friend and companion on the road to salvation. We could include wasting time with Jesus, silence and solitude with Jesus, acts of kindness with Jesus, time of sharing feelings with Jesus using all the senses and the arts, and could close with a birthday party for

Jesus with gifts which are expressions of ourselves, homemade, for those for whom Jesus comes—the poor, needy, hurt, oppressed. Gifts might be commitments to social actions that might change their condition rather than a specific gift such as food.

Epiphany: This could make a wonderful time to celebrate the three wise women, Mary, Elizabeth, and Anna. The celebration could take shape around their songs and their implications for our lives, for our pilgrimage toward salvation.

Lent: A series of events centered on the way or stations of the cross could be planned, beginning with a Shrove Tuesday Mardi Gras celebration that ignores all the evil and sin in the world and celebrates the goodness of creation, of food, drink, the body, the sensuous. The fourteen stations of the cross might be created by intergenerational groups in art, drama, and music, which relate each station to an identifiable sin in their community and world. The stations placed in different parts of the church or church grounds, the congregation might go on a pilgrimage along this way of the cross on one occasion or over a series of weeks.

Easter: On Good Friday the church could symbolically die, all symbols of the faith removed and a campfire lit outside the door or in the parish hall. The congregation could gather to sit around the campfire and through dramatization recall the story of the faith, dance the psalms, and sing songs of hope. This Easter vigil turns into an Easter celebration with the lighting of the Paschal candle from the campfire, and the procession back into the church for a celebration of its rebirth.

Pentecost: This would be an appropriate time to celebrate in the context of a church birthday party the power God gives us to live as a sign of and witness to God's kingdom. It is a time to reflect on parish life and to celebrate, evaluate, and commit the community to being a more faithful witness and sign of salvation.

Catechesis Within Rites of the Christian Year
Opportunities for catechesis within the seasonal celebration of the church are obvious. They include decorations, vestments, and

hanging, sermons and prayers, music, processionals, the presentation of the appropriate Scripture, and special events such as the Way of the Cross, footwashing on Maundy Thursday, imposition of Ashes on Ash Wednesday, Palm Sunday procession, Tenebrae on the Wednesday of Holy Week. Such dramatic events and festivals on saints' days or other special occasions provide ideal opportunities for catechesis of all ages.

EXAMPLE:

A group of interested persons in a parish might be formed to pick out special saints' days—a new day (Martin Luther King) or a less frequently observed old one (Julian of Norwich). The congregation would then study their lives and faithful witness, and plan for ways these could be remembered and celebrated within the context of the church's Sunday liturgy or as a special festival day.

Catechesis for Rites of the Christian Year
The corporate celebration of the church's year and the various festivals of the Christian story must become fundamental places where catechesis and liturgy merge. If the church does little more than celebrate its yearly cycle and saints' days, catechesis will be significantly addressed. For too long we have forsaken the most important means we have to transmit and sustain the Christian faith—the church's year.

Children, youth, and adults need to be involved in every aspect of the preparation and enactment of each feast. We need corporately to establish the central theological focus of each event in the church's cycle of days and seasons, and we need to integrate the celebration of each event with the daily experiences of people. We need therefore to build events both before and after the event itself so that all age groups may focus on making the celebration relevant to their personal and social lives. We cannot be satisfied with celebrating only a historical event; we need to relate each event to our lives both within and outside the church.

The arts will provide us with the basic means for preparation and celebration. Further, all ages must reflect on the significance of each event for their lives. Mindful planning and designing of such events is essential. We cannot afford to leave these occasions to chance or to assume that past means are satisfactory. The test of our festivals is in the lives they enable and empower us to live. Many of our celebrations will need to be reformed so that they make possible a worldly spirituality of individual and social witness to the Gospel.

We need to organize the church around its year if we are to grow in our identity as a community. That means that we must eliminate all those secular events that have crept into the church's year. Mother's Day, Stewardship Sunday, Missionary Sunday and the like may well have to go. This does not mean that our concerns for these human events and needs have to be eliminated. It simply means that we need to begin with the church's year and let it inform our human concerns. For example, mothers could properly be remembered on the feast of Mary, the mother of Jesus, or the visitation of Mary of the annunciation. Stewardship concerns might be celebrated on the festival of a saint such as Elizabeth, the Princess of Hungary, and Missionary Day might be connected with a festival of Willibrord or Wilberforce.

The Church Year: Rubrics

The celebration of various seasons and special days, along with the celebration of various saints' days, gives the congregation's worship a rhythm, a changing perspective, and a wide view of the Gospel. Too many clergy preach and celebrate a rather truncated Gospel which is victim of the minister or priest's personal whims and causes, or victim of the particular concerns and interests of the present age. The focus of the Eucharist every Sunday is upon the redemptive work of Christ. But that redemptive work is given a helpfully different coloring, different shading, a different perspective when it is celebrated in different seasons of the church year. Congregations who work for more frequent celebrations of the Eucharist, without more attention to the church year, may find that parishioners complain "we do the same thing every Sunday." The church year can help to enrich the Eucharist without obscuring its central focus on the redemptive work of Christ.

For instance, a Eucharist in Advent should have a different feel about it, should be participated in from a different perspective than a Eucharist at Christmas. One season is a season of expectancy and hope, the other a season of fulfillment and wonder. In the home, a Thanksgiving Day meal is different from a Christmas meal. The same family eats the same kind of food. But the day gives new meaning to their meal. The same dynamic can be at work in the meals of the family of God.

Leaders of worship and liturgy committees should explore ways to accentuate the various themes of each liturgical season. Decoration of the sanctuary, banners, hymns, prayers and responses—all should be carefully selected so that the meaning of each season may be expressed in worship. For instance, we must not destroy the Advent time of waiting and expectancy by rushing to sing Christmas carols and to decorate the church. The time of waiting has its own distinctive value, not only as a fitting preparation for the joy of Christmas, but also as a worthwhile spiritual discipline in itself. The Advent lections speak of the "people who dwell in darkness." It is a restrained time of waiting, silence, self-examination and preparation. Darkened interiors, periods of silence within the service, restrained use of color and decoration as well as restraint in music will add to the congregation's participation in this season. Then, when Christmas arrives, candles, bright, joyous music and a burst of color should greet the worshippers. An Advent Eucharist will tend to be more restrained, quieter, perhaps more preparatory and penitential than a Christmas Eucharist. The varying rhythm of the church year will help us all experience the varying rhythms of the Gospel.

While the use of changing seasonal colors for our paraments and liturgical vestments is helpful for the changing mood and focus of the liturgical seasons, churches should not feel bound by a rigid, legalistic color sequence. Historical study reveals that there was tra-

ditionally great local variety and congregational spontaneity in the
use of color. While the use of a fairly uniform color scheme unites
the congregation's time to the time of other Christians elsewhere,
it is conceivable that a congregation might have special days or
local celebrations which would require a special observance and the
use of special color. The present tendency is to return to the variety
and spontaneity which once characterized the church's use of color
and decoration, dark colors dominating preparation time, and light
colors festival occasions.

A primary way for people to find out who they are—or, more
importantly, who they wish to be—is to learn who people were
who went before them. The reading of biographies is understand-
ably serious business for growing children. All of us are edified as
well as identified by the people we seek to emulate.

Many Protestants are recovering the joy and helpfulness of saints'
days. While the central focus of our liturgy is always upon
Christ and Christ's work of redemption, there is an honored tradition of celebrating the witness of those Christians before us who
have responded, in word and deed, to Christ and his work. Few
Christians today would be in danger of "worshipping" the saints—
which the church has never advocated, but which late medieval
popular piety sometimes approached—and will find saints' days of
great help in their own spiritual pilgrimages. The "saints," in the
biblical sense, are *all* Christians who faithfully respond to the Gospel. Among these saints, the church has found it helpful to focus
upon certain men and women whose lives show forth that faithful
response in a particularly vivid way.

Celebration of the saints need not be a historical commemoration; rather, the saints can help make contemporary and particular
the Gospel, reminding us of how men and women before us have
lived out the demands of the Gospel in their times and places.
"Seeing that we are surrounded by so great a cloud of witnesses,"
says the Letter to the Hebrews, "let us now run the race which is
set before *us.*" Congregations may decide that one particular saint
particularly embodies their vision of the Gospel and joyfully celebrate

that saint's day each year. Children will enjoy some recounting or dramatization of a saint's life. We may wish to claim new saints to remember and lift them up in our services—Martin Luther King, the Grimké sisters, Cesar Chavez, or others. The saints help to particularize the Gospel, to visualize its life-changing power, and to confront the concrete demands of living out the Gospel mandate in our own time and place by celebrating how others have lived the Gospel before us. The Advent saints are all people of expectancy and hope—Isaiah's prophetic vision, Mary's servanthood, John the Baptist's voice in the wilderness. These traditional subjects of the Advent lections are the saints of waiting, the saints of hope in the midst of darkness, the saints of humble servanthood. Their witness gives us clues as to how we might spend our Advent days.

The three-year ecumenical lectionary gives us rich possibilities for the better integration of Scripture into our worship. Three lessons should be read in every Sunday service. The lessons could best be read by lay people who are qualified and carefully trained for the public reading of Scripture. The lessons may be interspersed with hymns and responses. Devotional-materials and church-school classes may wish to coordinate their Bible study and devotions to the weekly lectionary. When the worship of a congregation is ordered around the appointed lessons for the week, this enables worship leaders as well as the congregation as a whole to know in advance what the general direction of the worship will be. This means that musicians can now key their hymns, anthems, and instrumental music to the general movement of the service and can plan for a better integration of music, Scripture, and acts of worship. For preachers, use of the lectionary means that there are more published resources available for biblical preaching than have ever been present in the history of Christian preaching. Across all denominations, a worldwide, ecumenical systematic way of integrating Scripture into worship is the wonderful possibility which is offered to us by the lectionaries.

Finally, we are reminded, in our planning for worship on the basis of the church year, that the central focus of Sunday worship is upon Christ and Christ's work of redemption. The church has a long history of problems with the church year. In the Middle Ages, for instance, when a Saint's Day fell on a Sunday, the Saint's life and work sometimes tended to overshadow the life and work of Christ. But this was a problem in the composition of the liturgy rather than in the observance of Saints' Days themselves. Once again, the central focus of Christian time and Christian worship is upon Christ. During traditional penitential seasons like Advent and Lent, the preparatory, penitential emphasis of the season must not be allowed to overshadow the joy and redemptive emphasis of the Eucharist. Sunday is "Resurrection Day" regardless of the season.

However, we must say that in regard to the problem of obscuring the redemptive focus of Sunday, the danger lies more in those congregations who follow what we have called the "programmatic year" than in those congregations who have abused the church year. The following of the church year, along with the use of the lectionary for Scripture reading and preaching, are the best safeguards against inadequate understandings of Sunday worship or the truncation of the Gospel—as well as primary means of helping the congregation know *who* it is and *whose* it is.

· 4 ·

Personal Growth in Identity

This chapter may be controversial; it may, however, prove to be the most valuable chapter in this book. Earlier we discussed baptism and tried to make clear our conviction that baptism and baptism alone is the church's rite of initiation. Baptism is *the* sacramental beginning of the Christian life. It always has been and it always will be. Christian baptism alone establishes us as members of the church. Just as our natural birth establishes us as members of a human family, baptism establishes us as members of God's spiritual family. Baptism is the sacrament of belonging. Through it we announce that persons belong completely and fully to God and to each other in the church. Baptism can never be considered as just a first step in a lengthy process of initiation. It is all or it is nothing. In the sacrament of holy baptism a person, whether six weeks or sixty years old, is made a complete and permanent member of the church of Christ. There is no way to be only partially a member in Christ any more than one can be only half pregnant. There is no way to be a Christian one day and not the next. We can deny our Christian heritage as we can deny our human family but we cannot change the fact that we are Christians any more than we can change the fact of our biological parents.

Of course, there is value in a person's continual affirmation of the fact of his or her Christianity. That is the reason why the Episcopal Church has established that the covenant of baptism may be renewed by all Christians at least four times each year within the context of the Sunday Eucharistic celebration: at Easter to remind us that baptism celebrates death and rebirth; at Pentecost to remind us that baptism is the indwelling of the Holy Spirit (there cannot be two baptisms, one of water and one of the spirit separated in time and place); at All Saints' Day to remind us that baptism establishes us as members of the church and among the community of the saints; and at the Sunday after Epiphany (Jesus' baptism) to remind us that baptism is the way into ministry. On each of these occasions, whether there is a baptism or not, it is important that the congregation renew its baptismal covenant.

Throughout our lives, as we grow in our understanding, deepen our affections and reform our behavior, we need to remind ourselves who and whose we are as a baptized people. We need to grow in our identity. Baptism makes us Christians, initiates us into the body of Christ once and forever. This chapter therefore is not about initiation, but rather about growth in identity, also about those critical moments in our spiritual pilgrimage that need to be celebrated. Baptism is the church's rite of initiation. Confirmation, on the other hand, is a rite of identity. This chapter is about the latter.

It would take a book to outline the confused and conflicting history surrounding first communion and confirmation as they relate to baptism. Almost from the beginning different practices have existed side by side. In the Eastern Church, baptism, first communion, and confirmation have remained as an integrated rite conferred on children at birth by a priest of the church. In the Western Church these three became separated with the priest celebrating the rite of baptism at birth and the bishop celebrating the rite of confirmation at a later date. In time, first communion assumed a separate, sacramental status and was celebrated a number of years after baptism but before confirmation.

The Reformation brought about other changes. Baptism and the Lord's Supper were established as the only sacraments. While the radical reformers returned the baptismal-eucharistic-confirmation rite to its unity, establishing it as an adult rite, the continental reformers established a somewhat confusing system whereby baptism was celebrated with children, but first communion was denied until an age of accountability when, at confirmation, a formal profession of faith could be made. Confirmation and the necessary instruction which preceded it became, to all intents and purposes, the means by which the church maintained the necessity of an adult, responsible acknowledgment of the baptismal faith for "full" membership in the church. Indeed for some it appeared as if confirmation was the second half of baptism and necessary for membership in the church. Of course, in time confirmation and first communion were moved to a young age, long before any intellectual or responsible action could possibly be made. Similarly in the Anabaptist-Baptist tradition, baptisms were celebrated at younger and younger ages, thereby losing their effectiveness as an adult rite. It is almost impossible to sort out the confusions surrounding baptism, first communion, and confirmation, their historical justifications and theological rationalizations.

It is important to realize, however, that in every age the church made an attempt to maintain a faithful church of faithful members. It is not easy to maintain a Gospel of grace, grace which is a gift and by which alone we are justified, and the necessary free response to and acceptance of that grace and its implication for our lives. While always attempting to maintain the paradoxical nature of grace, historically some churches emphasized God's action and others the human response. The problem continues in our day and will always be with us. The church in every age must discern what it believes is God's will for maintaining a faithful community and helping people grow in their identity as Christians. We have our convictions. They are consistent with much Protestant and Roman Catholic thought today. We offer them to you for your consideration.

First, baptism alone makes us Christians and establishes us as members of the church. Baptism is normatively an adult rite, "adult" meaning no earlier than the late twenties. When celebrated normatively, baptism, confirmation and first communion are united and both God's gift of grace and our human response are celebrated. New rites of adult baptism and the necessary preparation of adult catechumens for baptism have been established. However, "normative" means that there can be and are legitimate and desirable exceptions. That is, children can be baptized if at least one of their parents is a faithful communicating, baptized adult who has participated in a serious disciplined period of preparation. These children, by their baptism, are complete and permanent members of the church. They therefore have the right to receive Holy Communion and indeed should, at least in the form of wine, at their baptism. We are further convinced that they should be present and participate in the weekly communion of the church from that day forward. Baptism is the only requirement necessary to receive the Eucharist. If we do not intend to permit a person to receive the sacrament we should be consistent and delay baptism.

We therefore recommend the eventual elimination of a "first communion" celebration. Catechesis for communion needs to take place during a child's first six years, while a baptized child is communicating, and is the responsibility of the child's parents as an aspect of their baptismal vows. The Eucharist is a holy *mystery*—perhaps only children can fully understand it. In any case, to "understand," we need first to *experience* it and *then* to *reflect* upon it. It is this reflection which needs to occur as a child matures.

For many, who are accustomed to the process of baptism, delayed communion, then "first communion" in early adolescence, our suggested pattern of baptism with communion will appear to be a radical suggestion. Our additional recommendation that the church establish a new *puberty rite of responsibility* may seem even more radical. But a puberty rite would allow confirmation to become a truly adult rite, a "sacrament" of mature commitment to mission, an "ordination" into ministry. But it is our conviction that our human spiritual pilgrimage, our growth in identity as Christians, has two significant turning points which need to be prepared for and celebrated. Much of this is provisional and necessarily vague, for it enters untested and unexplored territory. It is based, however, on our understanding of the spiritual journey in which faith appears to express itself through identifiable styles at different times in a person's life if necessary conditions are met.

Our Spiritual Journey

Typically, the style of a child's faith is *affiliative;* that is, *institutional, fiducial* and *heteronomous.* During childhood, faith is understood in institutional terms. As such, faith takes the shape of belonging participation and service in a community of faith. It focuses upon relationships and personal decisions in the realm of the feelings. It is expressed primarily through the affections or the responsive-intuitional mode of consciousness in the form of cultic life (symbol, myth, and ritual). Authority is external; that is, in the community and its tradition. It is concerned with conserving; traditioning is dominant. Affiliative faith is typical of children but when arrested in adults, it assumes the character of pietism, anti-intellectualism, and exclusivism.

Faith's maturation requires that those with the necessary potential be aided in moving to a new style of faith built upon these foundations. This new style can be characterized as *searching or ideological-intellectual-autonomous faith.* As such, it takes the form of questioning, first of others and then of self, by critical judgment of the inherited tradition and experimentation with alternatives. It is expressed primarily through cognition or the active-intellectual mode of consciousness in the form of doubt, rational investigation, and philosophical formulations. Faith is now understood in terms of belief and knowledge resulting from logical analysis. Its primary concern is right thinking and personal decisions on the basis of reason. Authority is now internal: that is, the self. It is concerned with prophetic judgment; retraditioning is dominant. Typical of late adolescence and early adulthood, when arrested in adults it assumes the character of agnosticism, rationalism, and anti-institutionalism.

If the needs of both affiliative and searching faith have been met, persons can grow into *integrated or mystical-performative-theonomous faith* which is best understood as the integrating of affiliative and searching faith. As a personal union with God, such faith is experienced through the integration of the intuitive and intellectual modes of consciousness in the form of a centered, integrated life of contemplation and action. Faith is now understood as obedience to

God's will. Its primary concern is right praxis or reflection—imaginative action. Authority is located in the unity of God and the self, and life is made purposeful by the integration of catholic substance and protestant spirit. By catholic substance we mean a concern for order, continuity, the conserving of the tradition and its judgment upon all human experience and reason; by protestant spirit we mean a concern for change, the prophetic judgment of the tradition by human experience and reason, and the transformation of the tradition. Only possible in the middle adult years, this integration assumes the character of a lifelong pilgrimage of growth and maturation.

In this faith pilgrimage two important crisis points usually emerge. The first comes in late childhood or between thirteen and sixteen. The second, in middle adulthood, or between twenty-five and forty-five. At present we have no liturgical or catechetical means for aiding persons in their growth in identity as Christians at these two significant moments. What follows are our recommendations for addressing this issue. But first a few thoughts about what we have called "adolescence."

"Adolescence" can only be dated from 1904. In that year, the American psychologist G. Stanley Hall wrote a book called *Adolescence*. Ever since, most people have behaved as if adolescence really existed. Margaret Mead and others have tried to help us understand that adolescence is not natural, not found across history and culture, but is rather a social construction of reality. To put it another way, adolescence does not exist except in our minds. Like psychosomatic illnesses, it hurts just as much as if it were biologically real; but it is important to realize that adolescence is only in our imagination, and therefore needs to be addressed accordingly.

Many of our problems in church and society as well as in the lives of persons and their families are related to the establishment of a lengthy period in which one is neither an adult nor a child. While this prolonged moratorium period may be economically necessary, we need not assume that it is socially and politically necessary. Perhaps many of our maturational and moral problems are related to our establishment of this unnatural state called adolescence. Perhaps it would be well for the church to live with only the categories of childhood and adulthood. At the appropriate age of sixteen, a physical, emotional, and behavioral transition point in human life, we might ceremonially move children into adulthood.

The need for a rite of accountability and responsibility seems obvious. We are a civilization without a true puberty rite or rite of passage from childhood to adulthood. Some people try to make confirmation into such a rite but it has failed. Instead of graduating persons into adult responsibility within the church, it has acted as a graduation exercise out of the church. First communion, connected with confirmation, tends, in Protestant churches at least, to be the last communion in many cases. Those who have had to live sixteen years of their life without the Lord's Supper will not be hard put to do without it for another sixty. They cannot miss what they have never come to love or need.

Similarly, asking a person to make a rational response and a commitment of faith at a time when he or she has at best only acquired the necessary cognitive ability to question and the freedom to seriously explore alternatives is to give the person the impression that he or she has already done that which he or she has not yet begun to do. Not only does adolescent confirmation (as we now celebrate it) arrest the growth of persons, it encourages them to believe that the intellectual quest is really unimportant.

More important, when we do not provide meaningful and appropriate rituals, ordeals, or vigils that the young must pass through to demonstrate that they can now be accepted as women and men among their elders, we encourage them to devise their own ceremonies. Our children therefore tend to revert to and pervert those ceremonies of adulthood found in our "primitive" collective consciousness, namely sex and pregnancy.

A Rite of Responsibility
The church must establish a rite of responsibility for our children (at about sixteen years of age), a rite of passage into adulthood.

The church, of course, must make major changes in its organization, life, and expectation if such a rite is not to be a farce. We will need to reorder our lives so that sixteen-year-olds can be elected in numbers to important decision-making groups, encouraged to serve on the altar guild and board of ushers, to be church-school teachers and lectors and leaders of prayers at the services of the church. They must be encouraged, aided, and supported in every aspect of adult life of the church. Of course they will not always be fully responsible. Who of us is? They will not always make wise decisions. Who among us does? But they will have the opportunity to learn what it means to be a responsible adult, what it means to be an accountable member of church and society. And we suspect, in a world which prevents them from growing up, they will seek out the church because it will take them seriously. More important, as "adults" given the responsibility of maturing in faith, they will be encouraged to question and doubt, to look critically at the faith they were nurtured in, and to strive to make sense of that faith. But they will do so within the church.

Adult Confirmation

Assuming that we have a new puberty rite of responsibility and accountability, the church will then be able to reconsider the place of confirmation. Until we have such puberty rites, children and their parents will fight to keep confirmation, not because it serves their needs, but because they know they need something. Without a desirable and useful alternative, they will attempt to save what they have. However, with a meaningful puberty rite, confirmation will no longer struggle to serve a function which is a denial both of its theological intentions and the human needs of persons.

For a long time we have talked about the ministry of the laity but we have neglected any serious catechesis or ritual to celebrate the call of persons to ministry. The only preparation we offer is three years of seminary and the only ritual we have is ordination to the priesthood. Further, we have no way to encourage or celebrate a person's growth into mature faith. By ignoring this crucial place in our human pilgrimage of faith, we arrest faith and estrange it from an adult's daily life. During our thirties and forties, crisis years in our identity quest, there is currently no significant way to unite faith and life, to make an adult commitment to faith and Christian ministry.

We, by our baptism, all share a common vocation or call to live in the spirit, to engage in a lifelong pilgrimage of sanctification. Our ministry is the means by which we express that baptismal vocation in every aspect of our lives. Our shared ministry cannot be adequately exercised in the free time, the leisure or volunteer hours people spend in and for the church. A ministry is not simply engaging in some means to earn a living with a Christian spirit, nor is it limited to certain ways of making a living which serve the institutional church or generally help people.

We need to learn and celebrate an understanding of vocation and ministry that is related to everything we do at work and play, in church and in the world, at home and outside the home, including the ways we earn a living and the ways we spend every moment of the day. We need to help persons discern their ministries, and prepare them to proclaim through deed and word their Christian faith through those ministries.

We need to overcome the split between secular and sacred and help persons to live out their ministries in the world. Confirmation, which could be thought of as a repeatable rite of baptismal renewal, is perhaps best understood as the "ordination" of all baptized Christians into their ministries in the world. Confirmation, as a unique rite of adults, could help the church remain faithful and encourage persons to take seriously their baptismal mandate and covenant as responsible ministers in Christ and members of his church. As a "sacrament" of the spirit, we could liturgically, catechetically, and pastorally stress the importance of the indwelling spirit, present with us since baptism, in our daily life as adult Christians. With the laying-on-of-hands and with prayer we could make it dramatically clear that Christian life, growth, and ministry requires the strength which God provides through God's spirit.

Through the establishment of a normative, unified *adult baptism-confirmation-and-first-communion rite* (with exceptions for child baptism-communion), a *rite of responsibility for adolescence* and an *adult confirmation,* we might meet the needs of a faithful church in our day.

Identity Catechesis
One of the most troublesome issues we face in relationship to all catechesis, but especially in terms of initiation and identity rites, is the nature of learning. There is a tendency for the church to assume that intellectual understanding must precede experience, an assumption which itself is a denial of human experience. If we must intellectually understand love before we fall in love, it will never occur. Action usually precedes reflection in human understanding. We make love in order to fall in love. We make believe so that we may believe. The early church knew this. An adult catechumen lived in the church for a period of years as a catechumen, so as to hear the Christian story and be encouraged to live as a Christian in the world. Only after a person's actions were judged Christian did the catechumen explore, during Lent, the church's rational attempts to make sense of its story and way of life. Indeed, it was only after a person's baptism and first communion on Easter that he or she reflected on the meaning of these holy mysteries during Eastertide. Learning best takes place in this manner; that is why catechesis is best understood as *experiential.* Learning moves from action to reflection. We move from the act of experiencing to the attempt to make sense of our experience. Catechesis begins by preparing ourselves to act, then we act, and finally we reflect upon that action and thereby make sense of it.

Further, catechesis has always acknowledged that *the mind functions through two modes of consciousness.* One mode is best described as a *responsive or intuitive mode.* It focuses on the affections (emotion) and experience. It is characterized by chaos, surrender, mystery, imagination, and surprise, and is nurtured by the arts and nonverbal activities. It is expressed through symbols, myths, and rituals.

The second is an *active or intellectual mode*. It focuses on cognition or thinking and reflection. It is characterized by order, prediction, logical analysis and control, and is nurtured by the sciences and verbal activities. It is expressed through signs, concepts, and reflective actions. The responsive mode relates to the experience of God and the life of prayers. The active mode relates to theological thought and moral decision-making. Both dimensions of consciousness need to be developed. Indeed, maturity assumes their development and integration. But the responsive mode is necessarily and always prior to the active mode.

Catechesis affirms and encourages the development of both modes of consciousness; it also takes seriously the order in which they precede. It is also important to note that liturgy functions primarily in the responsive mode as does preparation for ritual action. Reflection is a secondary activity which necessarily takes place after the ritual has been performed. Catechesis therefore is not only an activity which prepares us for participation in a ritual but an activity which takes place after the ritual has been enacted. When we plan for liturgical catechesis, it is best to begin with a ceremonial action followed by a catechesis of reflection on the ritual experience. For example, baptismal catechesis for adults begins with a ceremonial which establishes a person as a catechumen. Catechesis then takes place primarily in the receptive mode through symbol, ritual, and myth. Following this preparation the person is baptized at Easter and catechesis continues in the active mode of reflection on the meaning of baptism, and on the Eucharist and its implications for life. The rite ends at the following Pentecost.

Catechesis and Personal Growth
There are few more difficult problems for catechetics than confirmation. Most people are moved by nostalgic emotion. Few understand the historical or theological issue surrounding this rite. A major effort addressed to the whole church must be made if the communion of children and adult confirmation are to be realized. Even a more significant effort must be made if a rite of responsibil-

ity is to evolve and be accepted within the average congregation. Perhaps for a time we will need to maintain our present confirmation programs and offer alternative rites of responsibility and adult confirmation for those who are interested. In any case, before we can move in new directions we will need to develop a long-term catechetical program to prepare persons for such changes and to equip them to make these changes relevant.

EXAMPLE:

A yearly gathering with parents of eighth-graders to discuss the nature of the Christian pilgrimage and the needs and expressions of faith at various times in one's life. The group might also discuss various ways to celebrate their children's passage or pilgrimage; as well as what they and the church might do. A proposal for a rite of responsibility and catechism could be presented and interest established among some. Parents could then discuss these options with their children.

Catechesis for a Rite of Responsibility

A yearly series of inquiry sessions for children sixteen or over and their parents needs to be offered in order to determine whether or not children and their parents are prepared for this important step. These sessions should be followed by personal interviews with the children to ascertain if they desire to assume responsibility for their faith and conduct; they will also need help to establish who their adult sponsor will be—that is, who will aid them in their preparation for the rite of responsibility. When a sponsor believes the child is prepared for the rite of responsibility, the child would prepare his or her own rite of responsibility with the minister or priest.

Following this rite, those who participated would be enrolled in groups to engage in a program of catechesis to reflect on their experience, to acquire skills in Bible study and theological reflection, and to gain the necessary knowledge, attitudes, and behaviors for participation in some aspect of the church's life. The reflection could be done on a retreat following the rite and skills acquisition

first in informal and formal settings in the context of later participation.

A preparation program for adult sponsors will be essential if they
are to aid children, over an undetermined period, to explore the nature of the Christian pilgrimage in terms of their doubts and questioning; in terms of discipleship and the nature of responsibility for
self and society; in terms of their ministry in the church as a sign of
God's Kingdom; and in terms of covenant and promise.

Catechesis for Rite of Adult Confirmation

Periodically, inquiry sessions for adults could be held to establish
whether or not a person was ready for this important step. After
personal interviews, a sponsor could be named to aid the person
prepare for his or her confirmation.

In formal and informal session and retreats, each confirmand
could review his or her spiritual pilgrimage and reflect upon his or
her beliefs and those of the church. Confirmands would, further,
explore the spiritual rule of life in terms of prayer, Bible-reading,
and the practice of the virtues.

Once this has been accomplished, the confirmands would strive
to discern the graces in their lives, and the ministry or ministries to
which God was calling them. Parenthood is an occupation and
ministry, so is voluntary service in and outside the church. These
are all related to confirmation and ministry. Once this calling is
discerned, the rite of reconciliation and a rite of commitment of
Christian service could be celebrated.

Following these ceremonials, the confirmands would engage in a
lengthy period of formation for their particular Christian ministry.
Once this preparation is completed, they would be confirmed or
ordained to this ministry.

Later in life they may change their sense of God's call to ministry. The use of the new rite of Christian service in the 1979 Book
of Common Prayer could celebrate this new decision and bless it.
Before such an event, or simply periodically, retreats for those who
are contemplating a change in occupation or labor could be useful
to help persons discern God's will and ministry. Catechesis to help

persons make decisions and to prepare them to be faithful in their decisions is necessary.

Rubrics for a Rite of Responsibility
and Confirmation

Since a rite of responsibility does not currently exist, one must be developed. It is important that congregations design and experiment with various options until one emerges as valuable and relevant to the Gospel and persons. Some of the following elements should be included. The rite should be personal for each child rather than a corporate, group celebration. It should take place at the Sunday Eucharist, perhaps on or nearest the child's baptism day and should be seen in the context of baptism. The parents should present the child to the congregation. The child should write his or her own statement of a desire to participate in this significant event and what he or she believes it implies for the year ahead. The child should be given an opportunity to assume an adult role in the liturgy as a demonstration of his or her intentions. The parents might properly pray a prayer such as: "Thank you God for taking away from us the burden and responsibility of our child's faith and conduct." A symbol of the child's commitment should be given as a gift, perhaps in the form of a Bible and a medal of some Saint the child wishes to emulate.

The child should make a formal commitment to assume responsibility for his or her faith and conduct to engage in an intellectual quest to understand the faith he or she has been nurtured in. The congregation vows to support the child in his or her continuing pilgrimage and accepts the child as a full participant in the life of the congregation. The child is then commissioned to assume adult responsibility in the congregation through the laying-on-of-hands, and a party is held to celebrate that decision.

The liturgical core of the rite of confirmation should be the laying-on-of-hands with prayer for the gifts one needs to fulfill one's Christian vocation. Both our proposed rite of responsibility and confirmation should take place, if at all possible, in the service after a baptism but before the Eucharist.

· 5 ·

Spiritual Growth:
Daily Individual and
Common Prayer

Within Judaism the basic unit of time was the seven day week for which Genesis 1 indicated the liturgical significance in each day. Days were marked by a morning and evening sacrifice and corporate worship consisting of Psalms and prayers at nine in the morning and three in the afternoon. Devout Jews also marked three times of the day with private prayers, before bed, at rising, and at noon.

The early Christians organized each week around Sunday, the first day of the week, rather than around Saturday or Sabbath, the last. Each day, following Genesis 1, maintained a special significance, but each day took on a new meaning. Sunday was the day of creation; it was also the day of resurrection or new creation. Monday emphasized the unity of all life with God with Jesus Christ. Tuesday stressed dependence on God for life. Wednesday celebrated the conviction that all time and history belonged to God and that it was within history that Christ acts to bring into reality God's kingdom. Thursday focused upon our human unity with all creation and that the action of God in Jesus Christ was for all humanity. Friday reminded them of our human genesis and of the fact that we were all born to die. Saturday was a day of resting in the Lord and of patient, trustful waiting for the resurrection. Sunday was the day of resurrection.

While rejecting the sacrifice of the temple, the early church re-

87

tained the practice of marking each day with morning and evening corporate prayer. The morning service was a liturgy of the Word consisting of readings, instruction, and prayer. All who were able were expected to be present for this daily liturgy. Those who could not be present were expected to study the Scriptures and pray at this same hour wherever they were. The evening service which included psalmody, prayer, and readings was introduced by a blessing of the lights and sometimes was followed by a simple meal or *agape*.

In addition to these two public services (or private services held at corresponding times), other hours during the day were marked by private prayer. For example, the third, sixth, and ninth hours were associated with events of the passion. To these times two others were added: midnight—associated with the praise of God by all creation and the expectation of Christ's return; and cockcrow (dawn)—associated with the denial of Christ and the hope of resurrection.

In time, two systems of daily offices emerged. Originally known as "choir offices" (because they were led from the choir of the church rather than from behind the altar), they became, collectively, the "Divine Office" (a title reflecting the teachings of St. Benedict and others that the liturgy in the daily round of prayer and praise is best understood as the work of God). For a long time, daily morning and evening prayer for all Christians coexisted with a more elaborate sequence of monastic offices conducted every three hours: Matins at midnight, Lauds at 3:00 A.M., and Prime at six (the beginning of the day), Terce at nine (third hour), Sext at noon (sixth hour), Nones at three (ninth hour), Vespers at six (lighting of lamps), and Compline at nine P.M. (before bed).

By the sixteenth century, common daily morning and evening prayer had fallen into disuse. Luther gave a new emphasis to morning prayer by combining Matins, Lauds, and Prime into a daily office at the opening of the day and to Vespers, or the combination of Vespers and Compline, at the close of the day. Thus the Reformation hoped to reestablish the importance for all the people of the daily round of community prayer, praise, and the meditation upon Scripture.

At the beginning of the day, Luther maintained, it is important to remember that God will be with us all day directing our lives and sustaining us in our labor. At the close of the day he reminded us that we need to reflect on our faithfulness during the day past and to ask God to protect us through the night and bring us to a new faithfulness in the new day. Lutherans, Anglicans, and Roman Catholics have, to greater and lesser degree, maintained the importance of daily common prayer for Christian life; that is, of taking time each day to sing praises and thanksgivings to God, to listen to and reflect on God's Word to us, and to center our attention on God and recognize God's presence in our lives. Equally important, these traditions have maintained that we are corporate selves and need to pray with others; that we need to be supported and encouraged in our prayers by the presence of others; and that we need the community to pray with us, if our life of prayer is to be vital and not wither through neglect.

Free Church Protestants—United Methodists, Baptists, Presbyterians, and others—while not having a liturgical tradition of corporate daily prayer, nevertheless have long stressed the importance of individual daily prayer. The Methodists, for instance, as heirs of John Wesley, affirmed the importance of a "methodical," disciplined, personal prayer life. Wesleyans share with many evangelicals a long and recently renewed interest in small prayer groups which meet for group sharing and prayer.

The Recovery of Daily Prayer

In our own day, the Second Vatican Council authorized *Christian Prayer,* a new liturgy of the hours for common use. The new *Lutheran Book of Worship* has morning and evening prayer, complin, and suffrages for use during other times of the day. Similarly, the new Episcopal *Book of Common Prayer* (1979) has similar liturgies, as does the new *Presbyterian Worship Book.* The United Methodists are currently working on a Daily Office in their *Supplemental Worship Resources* series.

To spend a few days living in a religious community such as a monastery or convent or on a spiritual life retreat is to be transported into another world. There are many differences, but perhaps the most obvious is that time is ordered by hours of common prayer. In the secular world we are subject to the clock, but our sense of time lacks depth and is often without meaning. Our days are often dull and routine, our labor anesthetizing or harried. We often try to escape time through superficial partying or other activities aimed at dulling our sense of time. There is only the relentless existence of work time and Saturday night fever, a landscape where God is forgotten or only a memory. Our vacations (we do not commonly refer to them as holy days—holidays) do not provide an anticipation of what time might be; instead they only provide us with an escape from time.

The question remains, is it possible for the doctor, the teacher, the parent, the student, the parish priest, the factory worker, the business person, the show owner, and the rest of us to know in the disordered world of human affairs anything of that serenity and centeredness that we glimpse during a few precious hours spent on retreat? With duties to perform, trains to catch, and deadlines to meet, how can there be anything like a prayerful ordering of time? Is there any way to experience time in an alternative way to the sense of time by which we usually live? These questions are of course rhetorical. Those whose time is lived daily between the hours of morning and evening corporate prayer, whose lives are marked by moments for personal meditation, can indeed experience an alternative.

When our lives are caught up in time ordered by prayer, personal and corporate, we experience a reality quite different from the pressures and routines of our everyday experience. When we live by a prayerful ordering of time, we feel at home in the universe, and we experience a liberating serenity even in the midst of turmoil and trial.

How can there be a prayerful order of time outside the monastery or convent when we must also respond to the innumerable demands of family, work, neighbor, and community?

Persons living under the strains and stresses of the everyday world need, we contend, to find a rule of prayer that will be flexible enough to allow us to meet the incessant and unpredictable demands made upon our time and yet regular and firm enough to provide that spiritual order necessary for sanity and meaning. We know that we need such times, but we don't know how to find or make them. Typically we hear people say that they want to go to church on Sunday to find quiet peace. That is the reason people often give for not wanting children and the noise and confusion they bring at Sunday worship. That also explains why some don't want to participate fully in the service, but prefer to quietly listen and observe. What we seek is order, silence, and peace. These needs of course are real and important, but when we force our Sunday liturgy to meet these needs we distort the Christian faith. We forget that Saturday is the Sabbath day of rest. Sunday is necessarily a celebration day, a party day for families, an occasion for involved, communal, joyous participation. Monday through Saturday, on the other hand, are days for quiet personal meditation in communities. That is why daily public and common prayer is rightly considered among the primary duties of the church.

The church shares with many other modern institutions religious tasks common to all. There remains, however, one task, one prerogative and peculiar ministry which no other institution has claimed, the conduct of daily common prayer. Wherever and whenever people meet together for prayer, there is the church clearly and distinctly defined. Everything else can be conceded, compromised, shared, or even relinquished. If the church does nothing else for the world other than to keep open a house, symbolic of the homeland of the soul, where in season and out of season people can gather daily to pray, it is doing the social order the greatest possible service. So long as the church bids people to daily meditation and prayer and provides a simple and credible vehicle for the devotional life, it need not question its place, mission, and influence in the world. If it loses faith in the daily offering of common prayer, it need not look to its avocations to save it, for it is dead at its heart.

Nothing may be any more important than a rebirth of daily morning and evening common prayer in every church. Of course, the times will need to be arranged to fit the needs of particular communities. Day-care centers may be needed to care for children. Perhaps an early service for those on their way to work or school, and a later service for parents with children at home and older adults would be helpful. Noontime may prove to be best for those who work, or compline each evening with the church gathering at the close of the day. In any case, such services will necessarily need to be sufficiently brief, fifteen to twenty minutes, so that most people who are earnest about the matter will find time for them. It should be the urgent priority of every Christian community to restore a daily celebration of the hours to frame and inform our workdays. Only then will we have adequately responded to one of our era's greatest pastoral hungers.

Through common prayer we can experience time in a new way and we can be put in touch with the rhythms of a life lived with God, self, and neighbor. Through the psalms we can be drawn into the depths of human experience and express our deepest feelings. Through common prayers and songs we can gain a sense of communion and solidarity in a world of individualism and competition. Through the reading of and meditation upon the Holy Scripture we can make the Christian story our story, find an anchor for life with God in a world set adrift, and be confronted within the converting, transforming word of God. Through silence we can learn again to listen and hear God speak to our deepest needs in a world filled with noise. Through prayer we can bring our lives and the lives of others into the presence of God to be transformed and renewed, to be informed of and empowered to do God's will. Life and time are not endless circles in which we are trapped. Taking time to pray can make the time of each day sacred and our pilgrimage purposeful.

There is more, of course. Jesus commanded us to pray without ceasing, to live our lives continually in the presence of God, to be single-minded in our striving to discern God's will, to practice the virtues and be open to God's leading us to lives of service and action on behalf of human need. The celebration of the daily office can contribute to these ends, but we must also learn a personal spirituality as well. We are all on a spiritual journey. The ability to live a life of love for God and neighbor does not come naturally, though the human longing to do so does. The church is called to help us do so, to sanctify our days, thereby reminding us, "This is the day the Lord hath made, let us rejoice and be glad in it."

Spiritual Catechesis
The difficulties of reestablishing daily common prayer are numerous and great. Convincing the clergy that this is the best use of their time is among them. Finding the right time and being patient until the habit of regular attendance at common prayer develops are others. Our experience with theological students points up the problem. Even seminarians seem to find daily common prayer troublesome. There seem to be more pressing needs. Pastors find it embarrassing to tell their people that they will not be available on a particular day because they need to go on retreat to pray. For many it seems unreasonable to take time away from pastoral calls, committee meetings, study, sermon preparation, and other parish duties to pray. In our busy secular world it appears superfluous if not escapist. A concerted effort at catechesis will be necessary before common prayer can once again be considered a response to our common human longing for a spiritual centeredness. Further, catechesis will be necessary before common prayer can become a meaningful event in our daily routines.

Catechesis and Common Prayer
Most people would like an intimate relationship with God. We should apply what we know about human friendships to our friendship with God. For example, we like to be alone with friends. It doesn't matter what we are doing or whether we are doing anything at all—just to be in each other's presence is rewarding. Labor can be most satisfying when friends help each other. A task may be important, but when we do it with a friend it brings greater satisfaction. We can discuss issues with anyone, but when we share

with a friend issues are not all we share—we share our feelings, our hopes, our desires, our failings, our dreams. With friends we do not mind wasting time. When we are with a friend nothing important needs to be accomplished. There are times when friendships result in mountaintop experiences and times when they sink into valleys of despair, but most of the time life with friends is lived in the plains. Friends are perfectly willing to live in the plains. Our relationship with God needs to have characteristics similar to human friendship. Catechesis for daily common prayer can first of all help us develop a relationship of friendship with God.

For many people, praying is talking. We complain that God's presence is not very real and that we rarely hear God say anything. Of course, we wouldn't have a sharing, revealing relationship with other human beings if we treated them the way we treat God. Indeed, we wouldn't ever hear a friend say anything if we were never quiet enough to listen. We humans are so strange. Our seminarians go to chapel and from the minute they arrive to the moment they leave they talk, first to each other and then, when the service begins, to God. There is rarely a break in the conversation. Their prayers are all words spoken by them; they move rapidly from one Scripture lesson to another without even catching a breath. Silence is very unsettling. Many seminarians complain that even a few minutes of silence is almost impossible to bear. Catechesis can help us learn how to bear and use silence creatively, how to listen, and how to open ourselves to God's revelation of God's self.

Typically we hear people say, "We can pray by ourselves. We don't need others to pray. It is more convenient to pray alone." Perhaps we have had such thoughts ourselves. Individualism is a part of our life. We have been taught to go it alone. Yet, we long for community. Every church wants to be a friendly, caring community. We try to convince ourselves that we can pray best alone and at the same time we strive to find a means for creating community. We act as if we can be human alone, even as we long for meaningful relationships. Catechesis must help us learn that community is a gift given to those who pray together, who share life with God together, who share the longings of their hearts and the distortions of their lives with others in silence and in cries for help.

The daily offices are made up of psalms, canticles or songs, prayers, and lessons from the Old and New Testaments, and readings from non-biblical sources such as the writings of Calvin, Luther, Ambrose, Augustine, or spiritual writings by Ignatius, Teresa, Julian, or John of the Cross related to the scriptures or the special days which we are celebrating. Catechesis should help us understand the character and message of the Psalms. It will need to introduce us to the canticles and songs of the faith. It will need to help us learn to understand and interpret Scripture. A more important need is to help us learn to meditate upon Scripture. Through all this, we learn how to pray and what to pray for.

EXAMPLE:

A weekend retreat in which persons could experience the Divine Office with short preparation sessions before and reflection after each one. In the spaces between the offices, catechesis in meditation on Scripture and prayer could be conducted and practiced.

Catechesis Within Common Prayer

The primary catechetical event in the daily office is found in our confrontation with the Word of God in the Scripture of the Old and New Testament. The Scriptures ought not to be read dumbly. We must provide the congregation with background on the passages being read. Further, some comment on the context of the lesson should be provided. It is also important to have Bibles available for worshippers to follow the reading, but it would be wise to read from a different translation. For example, if the New English Bible is in the pews we might read from the Jerusalem Bible.

Equally important, silence must be provided after each reading, and it would be helpful in many cases to provide some guidance for meditation. For example, if the Old Testament lesson is Ezekiel 34:11–16, the congregation might be directed to reflect on their lives and recall a time when they were cared for, watched over, protected, nourished, saved, or found, to relive that experience and thank God for his shepherding grace in their lives. Another possibility is to read and reflect upon a short commentary on the lesson.

EXAMPLE:

A community of volunteer lay readers could be formed to read the lessons at services. An annual program of catechesis on Scripture, storytelling, reading, directed meditation, scriptural catechesis, and community prayer could be offered to equip them for this responsibility. During the year these persons could also organize and conduct short-term Bible study-prayer groups to meet in homes.

Catechesis for Common Prayer

In preparation for meaningful participation in daily individual or common prayer, persons need to learn the skills of spiritual discernment in prayer. The Bible provides us with two catecheses on prayer: Luke, written for gentile Christians who were learning to pray for the first time; and Matthew, for Jewish Christians who had learned to pray as children but whose prayers were in danger of becoming routine. Within both we have the Lord's Prayer or a summary of how and for what the disciples learned from observing Jesus at prayer. For all the Gospel writers, Jesus' prayer at Gethsemane provides the model: God, my parent, all things are possible for you, what do you desire for my life . . . Please God do not let this hour be among your givens, nevertheless your will be done for me . . . your will is given and received, praise be to you. We must learn what we are to ask God and how to listen to God's response; to learn to ask for what God instructs us to ask and to learn to have faith that what we have requested has already been given us.

The Lord's Prayer helps us to understand what we are to ask: namely, what do you want to make possible for me that neither I nor any other human being can make possible? What do you want to make holy in my life this day? How can God's kingdom come through me this day? What are my "Gethsemanes" about which I need to say "your will be done"? What nourishment or help do I need most this day? For what do I need most to be forgiven and whom do I most need to forgive? And from what do I need most to be protected? We need to learn to ask these questions and to listen to God's answers as preparation for common prayer. Further, we must learn the discernment of the spirits and to engage in it as preparation for common prayer. We must learn the habit of remaining conscious of our moods throughout each day and learn to discern their causes and meaning. We must make preparation for the day's prayers by the examination of our life experience and to discern where God's spirit is leading or calling us and what God wants to transform in our lives.

We must study the assigned lessons from Scripture with the aid of a good commentary as preparation for the daily office. We need to learn to make personal memory of God's manifestations or graces in our experience a habitual part of daily life so that we may return to drink at the springs of our graces at our common prayers. We can collectively formulate simple propositions on those issues in our lives which we have neglected to attend to or have not satisfactorily settled so that during common prayer we can take them before God and feel God's response. We must cultivate spiritual and psychological freedom from our hangups and addictions. We also need to seek a spiritual director to help us listen to the movements of our spirit and aid us in our spiritual journey. In that regard we should make occasional directed retreats to deepen our experience of God and the discernment of God's will for our life.

Once we have learned the skills of discernment, we can practice them as preparation for meaningful participation in the daily office. It seems like a great deal to learn; and it will require a significant amount of preparation. But once learned, it will be natural for us and provide the necessary ingredients for full and complete participation in daily life of personal and corporate prayer.

EXAMPLE:

While the two previous examples are applicable to catechesis for common prayer, short two- or three-hour noontime retreats could be held wherever people work. The group could fast so as to eliminate lunch. A short introduction to an aspect of prayer (such as that on the Lord's Prayer just discussed) could be given. Then persons could take an hour of silence to personally pray the Lord's Prayer, followed by sharing and common prayer.

Rubrics

Perhaps the most important thing to remember about the daily offices is that they do not require the leadership of clergy. Morning and Evening Prayer provide an opportunity for the laity to lead. Indeed, even if the clergy do provide leadership, the readings and prayers are properly led by the laity.

In preparation for each service it is important to investigate if the day celebrates some special occasion in the life of the Christian community. If it does, this occasion should be highlighted in a significant manner at the opening of the service.

Following the opening, a confession of sin is appropriate but not required. Following the absolution, an invitatory Psalm, the Venite (Psalm 95) or Jubilate (Psalm 100), is sung. Next comes the Psalm assigned for the day and then the two or three lessons assigned in the lectionary. These should be preceded by an introduction and followed by silence or directed meditation. Between the lessons, a canticle is sung. After the Gospel, a homily may be delivered or a piece from non-biblical Christian literature read. Next it is appropriate to recite together the Apostles' Creed. Then come the prayers. Time should be provided for individual prayers to be offered silently or, better, aloud. The service is ended with a blessing and dismissal. We cannot emphasize too strongly the use of the lectionary Psalms and the lessons from the Old Testament, the Epistle, and the Gospel each day so that over a period of two years the entire Scripture will be heard.

Sunday is a day of Eucharist, weekdays are for the daily office. Together they provide us with the nourishment we need to make our daily lives holy and transform secular time into God's time.

·6·

The Pastoral Offices:
Transitions in the Lives of
Persons and the Community

While baptism and the Eucharist are the norm, the basis, the context, the starting point for all of the church's worship, the church has traditionally celebrated a wide variety of other worship experiences which address the various stages of a Christian's life experience. These services are generally referred to as the pastoral offices. While they are not included in the Protestant list of sacraments, the pastoral offices are "sacramental" in nature—celebrating the presence and grace of God through the use of a wide variety of symbols and symbolic acts.

While baptism is sufficient initiation into the Christian community and while the Eucharist is sufficient sustenance for the community's life together, the church has found it helpful to offer her people additional opportunities for worship which are keyed to various points in the life cycle. These pastoral offices were not merely offered because people desired them or even because people were helped by them. As we said in the introduction to this book, the purpose of worship is the praise of God and nothing else. Christian worship is not to be *used* for the achievement of our human needs, not even the achievement of our very best human purposes. The pastoral offices were offered because the church found that various life crises provide excellent opportunities to proclaim the Gospel and affirm the faith. A man and woman marry, a woman gives birth, a person dies—all these events are wonderful opportunities for the community to gather for the affirmation and application of the faith to these significant turning points in human life.

Of course, while we are worshipping God during these changes, we assume that we are also helping people adjust and make meaningful the change. We trust that people are encouraged, educated, nurtured, disciplined, and sustained through their participation in the pastoral offices. We feel the pastoral care of the church in recent years has been preoccupied with a style of care which modeled itself on secular, one-to-one, psychologically oriented therapies. The second half of this book will speak about specific ways in which the church cares for people while the church is worshipping God.

Also, let us remind ourselves that, while we worship God in the pastoral offices, we are also educating people for Christian thinking and acting in the midst of life's crises. The chief purpose of the liturgy is not to educate people, but while people are worshipping God, they are also being educated in how the people of God think, feel, and act during life crises. In the pastoral offices, this education is not limited to the person who is presently going through some specific life crisis. We are also educating those who are preparing for a similar crisis in their future as well as those who may have been through such a crisis in their past. At a funeral, we are not only dealing with the grief, questions, doubts, and faith of the family who have suffered a bereavement. We also are dealing with the doubts, questions and faith of those in the community who are preparing for future grief situations as well as those who are still working through their unfinished grief from past bereavements. In other words, Christian worship maintains, even in the pastoral offices, its communal, corporate, ecclesial character.

Within every culture there are rites of passage, transition or life crisis to address the changes in people's lives. Some of these correspond to biological changes such as birth, puberty, and death; others correspond to social changes such as marriage, graduation, employment, retirement and the like. Such times of changed status and role are traumatic to both individuals and their communities. If we are to deal creatively and positively with life's transitions, if we are to understand the significance of change in our lives, liturgy and catechesis must once again be merged.

Our rites of life crisis help to make change meaningful in our lives, to restore order and harmony in the community affected by these changes, and to aid everyone, but particularly the next generation, to understand the meaning and purpose of change in human life. We cannot ignore the transition events in the human life cycle. The Christian faith has something to say to every negative and positive change in human life. Only when liturgy and catechesis take the human life cycle seriously will Christian life be made fully possible.

Rites of life crisis have three distinct phases: a separation phase marked by the ceremonial withdrawal of persons from their previous status, role, or state in the community; a somewhat lengthy transitional, liminal, ordeal phase in which persons are prepared for their new role and status; and a reentry phase which ritually establishes persons in their new status or role and reincorporates them into the community. In the light of these stages in life crisis rites, it should be obvious that catechesis is particularly applicable to the transitional phase. During this stage, persons are expected to acquire the foundational knowledge and understanding, sensibilities and attitudes, skills and behaviors needed to live purposefully and meaningfully in their new situation. Traditionally this learning is informal and experimental, but it is always taken seriously as the crucial aspect of the rite.

When we consider catechesis and the pastoral offices we need to explore what is necessary for a meaningful celebration of the rite as well as that catechesis which is integral to the rite itself. In that regard, it is important to note that the rite is a lengthy period and the ritual related to the rite a brief telescoping of the rite itself. For example, the rite of marriage begins at the engagement and extends until after the honeymoon; the ritual of marriage is the wedding ceremony. Unless the rite is handled adequately and fully, the ritual lacks full significance. While we need to consider the place that catechesis has within the ritual itself—for example, in the sermon at weddings and after the confession and before absolution in the rite of reconciliation—we must take very seriously the fact that catechesis is a dominant note in the rite itself. No longer can we afford to neglect the interrelations of catechesis and liturgy in the transitions in the human life cycle of persons and communities.

Particular events in our lives are so significant and touch us so deeply that it is essential for us to focus upon them in the light of our Christian faith. The purpose and function of the pastoral offices are to do just that. There is, therefore, no more significant and important place to integrate liturgy and catechesis than around these offices. The traditional pastoral offices related to "natural" human experience include concerns for marriage, birth, sickness, and death.

Other pastoral offices are related to times of moral crisis, vocational decision, and other disruptions in the community life. These offices traditionally include reconciliation and commitment to Christian service. New ones appear needed for occasions such as moving, divorce, and retirement. Still other pastoral offices, such as ordination and the celebration of a new ministry, are directly related to the calling of new symbol bearers for the community.

Each of these changes needs a Christian interpretation. Each presents the possibility of religious conversion to deeper faith and greater faithfulness. We shape and are shaped by our rituals. We are formed and transformed by our catechesis. Both liturgy and worship address the crisis points in the lives of persons and in the lives of their communities.

Christians look at and live in the world with God, with Christ. Christians affirm by faith that God is with them. They affirm that they can address God as *you* in what they call prayer. This may not appear to be a strange set of affirmations, but in the light of how many church folk act, it ought to appear strange. Many engage in the pastoral offices of the church and its sacraments as if they (each individually) must perform them as a duty required by God so that they can earn a reward after death. Or worse, they perform particular acts in order to receive from God benefits they would not or could not receive unless they did the acts. This is a magical view of the universe as contrasted with a religious view which contends that what we are doing is only and simply making real (actualizing) for ourselves what is already God's will for us. Surely, these sacramental acts convey grace. But instead of that grace being earned by the performance of an act, it is a free gift that we by faith (perception) and trust accept as already given. Of course, this trust or perception, this faith, is itself a gift for which we can only give thanks.

There is no way that catechesis can prove the presence of Christ in our lives or in these sacramental actions; there is no way to intellectually defend the belief that God's grace is a free gift which is only, but importantly actualized for us when we participate with faith in particular rituals; and there is no way to give persons the eyes of faith necessary for the realization of that previously given grace. All that catechesis can do is provide a context for the sharing of experience and for the reflection upon that experience. Still, this limited activity is essential or else a magical view of the universe will persist and Christian faith and revelation will be distorted in support of a sick religion of escape.

Let us now explore ways in which we educate and care for people within our celebration of the pastoral offices, speaking first of the origin and meaning of each of the offices, then reflecting on how we might prepare people for more meaningful participation in these offices, and finally thinking about how a congregation's worship leaders can give better leadership to these services.

·7·

The Celebration
and Blessing of a Marriage

The uniting of a man and woman in marriage provides an occasion for the church to involve itself in the most "corporeal" of all corporate actions. Marriage has to do with sex—procreation, physical love, union, and two individuals becoming "one flesh." Traditionally, the church has taught that Christian marriage also provides a relationship for mutual support and comfort of husband and wife as well as for the nurture of children. But even here, there is no escaping the utter carnality of it all; the mundane, worldly, fleshly, sexual quality of this pastoral office. And therein is its beauty.

The celebration and blessing of a marriage requires the church to act out the incarnational nature of its faith, to see the divine in the midst of human relationships, to affirm that creation, sexuality, and procreation are part of God's good scheme of things—gifts of a loving Creator who allows his creatures their part in his continuing creativity. For those who would make Christianity into an otherworldly, detached, "spiritual," individualized, ascetic thing, the celebration and blessing of a marriage is both protest and affirmation that ours is an incarnational, uniting, corporeal, and incorporating faith.

There is no service of marriage in the Bible. When marriage is mentioned in the Old Testament, it is seen in the light of two fundamental Old Testament convictions: God's creation is good, including God's creation of male and female and attendant human sexuality; and God's steadfast, covenant relationship with Israel is the model for all human relationships, including relationships between men and women in marriage.

While the Old Testament has a great deal to say about sex, including strict regulations for the expression of human sexuality, nowhere does the Old Testament imply that sex is evil. "God created man in his own image, in the image of God he created him; male and female he created" (Gen. 1:27). Sex is part of God's created scheme of things. It is the means by which human beings participate in the mystery of creation. But, like other aspects of human creativity, sex can be abused by humans, perverted and cheapened. While sex is to be entered into joyfully and with the knowledge that this is one of God's gifts to us, it is not to be entered into without due respect for the proper use of God's gifts.

Out of this concern arose Israel's conviction that sex was most helpful and most congruent with God's purposes when practiced in the context of a caring, faithful, creative, exclusive relationship, much like the relationship Israel enjoyed with her God. Old Testament writers frequently compared God's *hesed,* God's "steadfast love" for Israel in the covenant, with the way love should be for a man and woman in marriage. Just as God had chosen, loved, endured, and been faithful to Israel throughout the vicissitudes of Israel's national life, so married men and women were to be faithful to one another throughout the vicissitudes of human life. Conversely, the total, committed, self-giving love which men and women experienced in marriage was seen as a human analogy to the self-giving, total love which Israel received from her God.

The New Testament depicts Jesus as deepening these inherited Jewish concepts of marriage. When asked about marriage after divorce (Mark 10:11–12, Matthew 19:3–9, Luke 16:18), Jesus asserts that not only is marriage to be an exclusive and monogamous relationship but also that it is to be a lifelong relationship. The Pharisees then pointed out to Jesus that, under the terms of Deuteronomy (24:1), divorce was generally permitted, on the initiative of the husband, without stigma or litigation. There appears to have been much disagreement among the rabbis over what circumstances were sufficient cause for divorce. Some permitted divorce for religious reasons (Ezra 10:3, 44), or childlessness (Malachi 2:15). Some rabbis even allowed a man to divorce his wife on the basis of her bad cooking! Obviously, the woman's position in this arrangement was extremely vulnerable.

Jesus makes clear that he sees it differently:

> "Have you not read that he who made them from the beginning made them male and female, and said, 'For this reason a man shall leave his father and mother and be joined to his wife, and the two shall become one flesh'? So they are no longer two but one flesh. What therefore God has joined together, let no man put asunder." They said to him, "Why then did Moses command one to give a certificate of divorce and to put her away?" He said to them, "For your hardness of heart Moses allowed you to divorce your wife, but from the beginning it was not so. And I say to you: Whoever divorces his wife, except for unchastity, and marries another, commits adultery."
>
> (Matthew 19:3–9)

In other words, the church understood that Jesus considered marriage to be a permanent relationship as well as a relationship which took precedence over other human relationships, even the relationships of parents to children. Jesus is here putting forth an exalted view of matrimony, a view which sees marriage as part of God's created order, God's unifying purpose in creation; sees marriage as an example, a paradigm of the highest and most enduring of all human relationships—a relationship not unlike the relationship between God and his people. Paul underscores this theme:

> Wives, be subject to your husbands, as to the Lord. For the husband is the head of the wife as Christ is head of the church ... Husbands, love your wives, as Christ loved the church and gave himself up for her ... Even so husbands should love their wives as their own bodies.
>
> (Eph. 5:22–23, 25–28)

At first glance, Paul's statement on marriage appears to put forth a view which supports the subjection of women in marriage. But a closer look is required. Subjection is the primary principle here, but it is *mutual* subjection. It is mutual self-giving which is based, not upon vows, or compatibility, or even love, but upon the relationship of the husband and wife to Christ. For Paul, the nature of Christian marriage is derived from the nature of our relationship with Christ who reveals to us the true intended nature of our relationships with one another. This "mutual submission" is also enjoined in I Peter 5:5, Romans 12:10, and Philippians 2:3.

Any claim for male domination which attempts to base itself on this passage from Ephesians does injustice to the peculiar nature of Jesus' lordship as depicted in the Gospels. The Christlike "lordship" which Paul demands of husbands is the "lordship" of service, mutual submission, suffering, and total self-giving. Particularly in the context of Paul's day, this passage is far from being a rationalization of male dominance. Rather, it is a radical new image for male-female relationships in marriage in which the marriage bond is transformed from one in which the wife is simply subjected to the husband without qualification into one in which the husband is to devote himelf unreservedly in love for his wife. Perhaps "mutual devotion" is a more accurate interpretation of Paul's thought here than mutual submission.

In any case, it is clear that the model for Christian marriage is Christ's unreserved self-giving love. This is why the church has traditionally viewed the marriage bond as permanent, exclusive, faithful, and long-suffering. The love of God in Christ is our model, our example, our standard.

How is it possible for a man and woman to live in a lifelong totally committed relationship? How is it possible for the love of two people to endure all the trials, tragedies, and changes in this life? Such self-giving love would be impossible were it not for the church's claim that God's grace helps us keep our promises, endure the difficulties, and remain faithful. Little wonder, then, that when Paul thought of the sacredness of Christian marriage, he could do no better than to call it a *mystery*.

The service of marriage is a relative latecomer to the church's worship. In the early church, it seems that marriage ceremonies took place in accordance with existing local customs and local sanctions regarding matrimony. Then the church blessed the union, usually at some point in the worship service on the following Sunday. No full service of Christian marriage is found until the ninth century. When the church finally assumed oversight for marriages, it did so as a civil authority, church and state being viewed as one by this time.

As with many other liturgical acts, the church simply adopted local customs regarding rites of marriage and put them in a Christian context. Quaint customs like the bride's feeding the groom the wedding cake, the giving away of the bride, the throwing of rice, and the exchange of rings all related to earlier Roman and medieval customs. Much of the language of our traditional wedding services such as "to have and to hold" and "till death us do part" is legal terms that relate to property rights and legal contracts between two people and reflect the legal, civil origins of much of the marriage rite.

Today, when Christian ministers oversee the vows of a man and woman in marriage, they function, in effect, as civil officers, officially witnessing the vows in accordance with the requirements of a marriage license which has been issued by the state. In some cases, a couple may be married by an officer of the state (a Justice of the Peace or Judge) and then have their marriage blessed in the church. When they do so, they are participating in a custom which is very close to the practice of the early church. In the new marriage rites of various denominations, there is a growing inclination to separate the two traditional aspects of the church's dealings with marriage: the celebration of a marriage and the blessing of a marriage. This enables the church either to combine the two aspects in a full service or to simply bless a marriage which has been made previously before civil authorities.

From the beginning, the essence of the service of marriage was a contract freely consented to before witnesses. In the fifteenth century, the Council of Florence agreed that "the efficient cause of marriage is regularly the mutual consent uttered aloud on the spot." Most traditional Protestant marriage services have their roots in the old *Book of Common Prayer* which merely adapted the medieval services of marriage. The marriage service was altered less by the Reformation than any other rite. In these traditional services, as well as the new rites for marriage, we discern four main parts:

First, the service begins with an *Exhortation.* This tells the congregation what is going to happen and why the church is doing this service. In the exhortation, biblical passages on marriage may be quoted as well as some traditional statement on the purpose of the marriage bond. The *Book of Common Prayer* now says it this way:

> The bond and covenant of marriage was established by God in creation, and our Lord Jesus Christ adorned this manner of life by his presence and first miracle at a wedding in Cana of Galilee. It signifies to us the mystery of the union between Christ and his church. . . .
>
> The union of husband and wife in heart, body, and mind is intended by God for their mutual joy; for the help and comfort given one another in prosperity and adversity; and, when it is God's will, for the procreation of children and their nurture in the knowledge and love of the Lord.

Second, there is a *Declaration of Intention.* Early in the service, the man and woman state why they are present, their free and mutual consent to be married. This is not the vows; they come later in the service. In the declaration, the couple should express, without reservation, their intention of lifelong fidelity and acknowledge the responsibilities of family life. In expressing their intent, the couple should speak to the gathered congregation and witnesses, using the couple's Christian or first names.

After the declaration of intention, the congregation usually promises to uphold the couple in this relationship, verbally or symbolically expressing their commitment to this intended marriage. This part of the service reminds us that marriage is always a public affair, an individual act with social consequences. It is too difficult and too important a thing to be left exclusively to two individuals.

Other additional worship activities may take place in this part of the service. While these activities are not essential, normative parts of the service, most congregations find them helpful. Some may wish to retain the "giving away" of the bride—although this is a questionable vestige from a time when women were considered to be property of the family. The new United Methodist service suggests that this moment be used for both the bride's *and* the groom's families to state their blessing upon the marriage. Scripture lessons may be read at this point, along with a sermon, creed, hymns, testimonies from the congregation and other acts of worship which are familiar to the congregation in any service of corporate worship. Many congregations that formerly viewed the service of marriage as an abbreviated, individualized "performance" of vows between bride and groom before a minister now show a new interest in making the celebration of marriage into a full, multifaceted service of worship which more closely resembles their usual Sunday services. This enables the congregation to underscore the wedding as a service of corporate Christian *worship*.

Then the couple make their promises to one another, the *Vows,* taking each other's right hand and repeating those familiar words, ". . . to have and to hold from this day forward, for better or worse, for richer or poorer, in sickness and in health, to love and to cherish, until we are parted by death." The vows should express an unconditional commitment to a lifelong covenant. Once again, Christian or first names should be used. The vows are the central activity of the Celebration of a Marriage, the central, symbolic action of the couple in marriage. After the vows, rings or other visible signs of love and commitment may be exchanged. But these are optional appendages to the central activity of promise-making.

Finally, the service contains concluding prayers and the *Blessing.* If a couple is married outside of a church by some civil authority, then the blessing would be the only part of the rite which would be done in a service. The *Book of Common Prayer* provides a special service for the blessing of the couple in the union as the essential, central, symbolic, irreplaceable activity of the church in a marriage (other than the church's witnessing of the couple's vows). As we noted earlier, the blessing is the oldest aspect of the church's liturgical dealings with matrimony.

After the blessing, the service may proceed into the peace, the Eucharist (a particularly fitting way to celebrate the blessing of a marriage), or the couple may simply move through the congregation to greet those who have shared in the service. Or this greeting may follow a full Eucharist.

We suggest the following norms for the celebration and blessing of a marriage:

• The blessing of a marriage is the central, historical activity of the *church* at the time of marriage. In so doing we recognize marriage as a part of God's intended scheme of creation and as a noble Christian vocation. The service should clearly accentuate blessing as the central liturgical action related to marriage. The blessing is an affirmation that God's grace is needed for success in marriage and that God's grace is freely given to those who faithfully, sincerely, and commitedly enter into union with another person.

• From the beginning, the central activity of a *couple* in marriage is the exchanging of vows before witnesses. A public declaration of lifelong, unqualified, exclusive commitment is required for the actual making of a Christian marriage. Sometimes vows may be made before civil authorities. In this case, the only duty of the church is to bless the marriage. When a marriage is celebrated in the church, the church will usually have some firm ideas about the form and content of the vows. While in some denominations couples are free to write their own vows, the vows must be written in such a way as to express the *church's* commitment and belief about marriage—not just the individual couple's idiosyncratic understanding of marriage. When the *Book of Common Prayer* gives couples directives for composing their own liturgies for marriage, it says the vows are the only part of the service which cannot be changed.

• The celebration and blessing of a marriage is an act of worship of the Christian church. It is not to be a private, individualistic affair—any more than any of the church's other corporate gatherings are to be private and individualistic.

While it is true that our gathering is occasioned by the union of a specific man and woman, and while the rite will want to give expression to the specificity of who they are, we must not forget that the service of marriage "belongs" to the *church*. The bride and groom may wish to modify the service to give special expression to some special aspect of their relationship, but the service must be more than "their" private service. Since it is a service of corporate worship, we must judge the adequacy of our marriage liturgies, using the same criteria as we would to judge the adequacy of any other service of worship. We will have more to say about this in the rubric section of this chapter.

Catechesis and Marriage
We wait much too long to begin marriage catechesis. By the time a couple has decided to get married, catechesis is difficult. While we would not want to recommend a particular age, we are convinced that the church needs to help its children, youth, and adults deal with sexuality.

Defining sexuality as the ways in which male and female persons relate to each other and themselves, we contend that sexuality education needs to be an integral aspect of all catechesis. Sexuality is at the center of our being. We are born sexual, but we all need to explore the many and often confused facets of our sexuality and learn to celebrate this God-given gift so that it becomes an occasion for grace and not for sin.

Regrettably, education in sexuality has for too long been a controversial issue in the church. Not only have we dealt inadequately with sexual identification and sexual intercourse, we have ignored a healthy and holistic understanding of sexuality. Self-fulfillment as persons is not limited to marriage. While singleness in community is the norm for human life, marriage is the vocation for some Christians. Marriage is not the only faithful way by which men and women can faithfully relate to each other. Marriage catechesis needs to help persons answer questions such as: Is marriage necessary? What are the alternatives to marriage? Why should persons marry? Who should marry? What is the relationship between love, sex, and marriage? What is the relationship between marriage and parenthood? We need to help persons explore alternatives, to manage and consider the grave seriousness of entering into a marriage covenant. Singleness makes possible complete devotion to social ministries of justice.

Love is a necessary but not sufficient condition for marriage. One fundamental purpose of marriage is the procreation and nurturing of children, another is the support and assistance of spiritual growth and development. The latter being prior to and necessary for the former. A marriage should be consummated because both parties agree that they can better grow in grace and work out their salvation together than in any other manner or with any other person. Catechesis, beginning with children, must be developed. Needless to say, we have not even begun to contemplate what such catechesis in the church might look like. First, however, we will need to be convinced that it is necessary. Until we do, marriage will remain a secular institution entered into unadvisedly and lightly.

Our human goal for life is life in the spirit and ministry in the world. Marriage is one way, but not the only way, to express this vocation and ministry. However, if marriage is to serve this important function throughout our lifetime, marriage catechesis for married couples must be developed. Such catechesis after five years of marriage, or the mid 30's, and 40's, and 50's, will be especially important.

Catechesis Within the Marriage Rite

When the church encourages or permits a wedding without a full communal Eucharist of Word and sacrament, catechesis is made much more difficult. It seems to us essential that the marriage rite include the reading of Holy Scripture and homily on the texts. Non-biblical Christian readings can only be accepted if they are complementary to the lesson from the Old and New Testaments. Music must also meet these criteria. The homily should be seen as an opportunity for the catechesis of all children, youth, and adults who are present, and to help single and married persons gain a deeper understanding of the sacramental character of marriage.

Further, while a pictorial record of the marriage ceremony is typically made, it would be well to make a verbal recording of the total ceremony so that the family can at least on anniversary occasions recall and reflect upon this dramatic step in their spiritual journey.

Catechesis for Marriage

Premarital catechesis should focus on the spiritual aspects of marriage and the spiritual health of those preparing for marriage. Retreats, which aid the engaged couple, over a period of months, to explore their spiritual pilgrimage and equip them to help each other in their devotional life of prayer, meditation on Scripture, and discernment, are minimally essential.

Opportunity needs to be given to the couple to review the church's rite or help to prepare their own ceremony consistent with the church's teaching on marriage. Every word of the text and every promise to be made should be discussed so that both persons share a common understanding of the church's convictions about marriage.

Both persons must be helped to explore their vocation or spiritual life, and to discern the ministries to which God is calling them so they may support each other and grow in grace together.

In the Episcopal tradition, the priest is required, before the ceremony, to have the couple sign a statement which reads: "We, A.B. and C.D., desiring to receive the blessing of Holy Matrimony in the church, do solemnly declare that we hold marriage to be a lifelong union of husband and wife as it is set forth in the liturgic forms authorized by this church. We believe it is for the purpose of mutual fellowship, encouragement, and understanding, for the procreation (if it may be) of children and their physical and spiritual nurture for the safeguarding and benefit of society, and we do engage ourselves so far as in us lies to make our utmost effort to establish this relationship and to seek God's help thereto." Discussion and interpretation of such a statement can provide a helpful element in premarital catechesis.

Last, we believe that it is important for the couple to agree that after a period of about six months, they will attend with other newlyweds and married couples some specific number of sessions to reflect on their marriage, to explore the issues and problems they face, and to help each other fulfill their marriage covenant.

Marriage Rubrics

Perhaps more than any other act of corporate worship, the celebration and blessing of a marriage invites personal choices of its participants. As we noted earlier, from the beginning this rite has been heavily influenced by local custom and taste. This is an intensely personal, incarnational affair. At the same time, care must be taken in the leadership of this service because marriage is also a legal act which is subject to the laws of the state as well as an act of public worship which is subject to the beliefs of the church. In the past, great confusion has arisen in regard to the marriage service because of the misguided idea among many that the service of marriage is the "property," so to speak, of the bride and groom or their parents. The service of marriage, like all of the other services of the church's worship, "belongs" to the *church*. While the individual couple's personal tastes and desires may inform the service, the final content, direction, and purpose of the service are to be determined by the church.

The best time to celebrate or to bless a marriage is in the normal Sunday service of the congregation. When this is done, there is less confusion over whether or not this is a service of worship and less temptation to make the wedding into a private rite or a public spectacle. However, because of logistical problems, difficulties in assembling the couple's families and friends, or the sheer number of weddings in some parishes, marriages may be celebrated at another time than in the Sunday service. Even when marriages are celebrated elsewhere, at other times, it is a good idea to give the congregation the opportunity to bless the marriage during the next Sunday service. This practice helps to underscore the social, communal, and familial connotations of matrimony.

As with other services of corporate worship, the church is the best place to celebrate or to bless a marriage. Once again, there is less confusion over whether or not this is a service of worship when the service is conducted within the sanctuary of the church. Special liturgical banners, candles, and other limited decoration may be used for the marriage. But congregations should avoid too many flowers, candles or other adornments which clutter the worship space and which tempt florists and wedding directors into redecorating the sanctuary with costly and unnecessary superficial adornments which obscure the focus of the wedding. Likewise, the church's regular liturgical colors should be used rather than changing them to white. This sets the wedding in the context of the liturgical year and the church's normal worship patterns. Photographers, professional or otherwise, must be asked not to take flash pictures or to move about in front of the congregation. If ushers are used, they could ask guests carrying cameras not to take flash pictures during the service.

As for the service itself, the actions related to the celebration and blessing of a marriage, we have these overall suggestions. Maximum congregational participation should be encouraged through the use of a printed wedding bulletin (particularly when there are many guests who are not members of the parish). Music should be selected in close consultation with the church's music leaders. Congregational singing is to be encouraged, maudlin solos or performances by the choir are to be discouraged. Secular music, if it is requested by the bride and groom, should be used at some time other than the service. A general guide for planning and leading the service is to use the same standards and guidelines one would apply to any of the congregation's other services.

Here is a full order of service, a pattern, which is suggested in the new *United Methodist Service of Christian Marriage:*

GATHERING
- Entrance
- Greeting
- Declaration of Intention and Consent
- Response of Families/People

MINISTRY OF THE WORD
- Prayer
- Scripture and Praise
- Homily/Sermon
- Intercession

THE MARRIAGE
- Exchange of Vows
- Blessing/Giving of Rings
- Declaration of Marriage
- Response of Wedding Party/People

THANKSGIVING: (three options)
- Thanksgiving and the Lord's Prayer
- Holy Communion
- Agape Meal (Love Feast)

DISMISSAL WITH BLESSING
- Dismissal with Blessing and the Peace

This pattern provides an optimum amount of congregational participation as well as a structure for the service which closely resembles any full service of public worship. It suggests, as we did for the Eucharist, that worship is a pattern of actions which allows for possible variation in the words of worship rather than a fixed text of prescribed words.

A few notes on the pattern:

The GATHERING takes seriously that things must be done in order to gather and prepare people for true participation in worship. This would be a good time to greet out-of-town guests or to rehearse the congregation for their responses if unfamiliar responses are being used. The declaration of Intention and Consent is an essential part of the service, declaring to the gathered congregation that the bride and groom have freely consented to join together in wedlock. As with the other parts of the service, this may be a formal, printed response, or it may be more informal—a time when the bride and groom simply express, in their own words, their consent and intention to be joined together. The couple should use their Christian or first names. The Response of the Families may take the form of the traditional "Giving Away of the Bride," although a more appropriate response may be statements or actions on the part of each family which show the family's support for the proposed union. This is also an excellent time for the congregation, as a group, or as individuals, to publicly affirm its support of the bride and groom in this act of matrimony.

The **MINISTRY OF THE WORD** has been neglected in many of our traditional services. This is a time for the couple and the congregation to be instructed in the church's teaching regarding marriage, to hear the Gospel proclaimed in the context of marriage, and to celebrate the living Word which creates union and communion among God's people. Dance, drama, music, prayer, and poetry are all possible ways to engage and be engaged by the Word at this point in the service. Normally, this part of the service should be done briefly, so as not to destroy the momentum of the service or to unnecessarily prolong the duration of the total service.

THE MARRIAGE is the actual celebration of the marriage, the core of the marital rite itself. Here, vows are exchanged. The vows are exchanged as response to the Word of God. Traditional or original vows may be said as long as the vows have been formed in careful consultation with the pastor whose duty it is to ensure that the particular beliefs of the church's tradition on marriage are upheld. Any promise-making related to marriage must be phrased in simple unconditional terms which express a lifelong commitment to marital fidelity. Once again, Christian or first names should be used. It has become customary in many parishes for the vows to be said individually, by the bride and groom, facing one another, since their pledge is to one another, not to the minister. Their hands should be joined. The congregation joins the minister in witnessing the vows.

If rings are used after the vows, the giving and receiving of rings is then blessed. The minister declares that a marriage has taken place. After this declaration, members of the congregation or members of the wedding party may wish to make some response to the marriage—statements, songs, prayers.

The THANKSGIVING may be a final prayer of thanksgiving followed by the Lord's Prayer or the Eucharist.

The Eucharist is a very ancient way to celebrate a marriage and, as a sign of love and union, it is particularly fitting. The couple may present the gifts of bread and wine for the Eucharist, or one of the family or wedding guests might offer the gifts. We recently participated in a wedding in which the bride's parents presented bread which the bride's mother had baked and then the parents assisted the priest in distributing the bread to the wedding guests at the communion. By the way, if the Eucharist is celebrated, it must not be offered to the bride and groom alone. The Eucharist is never a private matter. It is the right of the entire gathered people of God. The United Methodists also suggest that some form of the ancient "Love Feast" or *agape* meal might be used rather than the Eucharist. We feel this is a questionable suggestion which could confuse the Eucharist with the *agape*. A nuptial Eucharist is the most fitting way to end the liturgy of marriage. This would depend on congregational tradition and on the couple's wishes, in consultation with the pastor and/or worship committee.

The service concludes with the DISMISSAL AND BLESSING. After the service is ended, the state license and church certificate and registry should be witnessed and signed by all parties unless this was done during the service (i.e. after the declaration of marriage). A joyful procession could then lead all the worshippers to a reception, wedding party, or picnic.

The tone of the service is one of joy and thanksgiving at the work of God in our midst, bringing a man and woman together, in spite of all the things which separate us. The pastor can do much to make guests feel welcome at the service and to ensure that the preparation of the service as well as the service itself is a witness to our beliefs in marriage. Each congregation, possibly through its worship or liturgy committee, should carefully consider its beliefs about marriage and should compose a set of congregational guidelines for weddings. Members of the committee should assist the pastor in educating couples about marriage and in helping the couple plan the wedding.

In a world where relationships between men and women have been problematic, where union between persons is increasingly difficult and demanding, where commitment to another person is too often short-lived and self-centered—Christian marriage has become one of the most missional, evangelistic, and confessional of the church's rites. Our careful planning, education, and leadership for this rite can ensure that our celebration and blessings of marriage are also times of witness, proclamation, and enactment of the love of God in our midst.

·8·

Recognition of Divorce

The church has been given the awesome power to loose as well as to bind. The church exists not only to bring persons together but also, on some occasions, to recognize and pray for separations among persons. Throughout the church's worship, we move in the space between our dreams and hopes for an ideal world where all are one in Christ and our honesty and realism about the temporal world where there are painful divisions and separations.

We hope it is clear from the preceding chapter that we believe that the church has a strong, bold, clear word to offer a man and a woman at the time of marriage. But we are convinced that the church should be equally bold and realistic in offering a word to fellow Christians who may go through the painful separation of divorce.

We do not mean to "bless divorce," as we have blessed a marriage, for we do not believe that it is legitimately within the church's authority to "bless" estrangement and breaking of promises.

However, we do mean to say that the church has a legitimate, biblically grounded, pastoral word to speak to persons whose lives are touched by the trauma of marital separation. The greatest tragedy of all would be for the church to say nothing.

In the past ten years, the divorce rate in the United States has doubled. In dealing with those among us who are going through the trauma of divorce, it appears that the church has two options: We can decide that divorce is an unforgivable sin or unpardonable offense, and then excommunicate all those who choose to divorce.

Some churches have tried this option. It manages to keep our stance on marriage firm. It keeps the church out of firsthand involvement in all those perplexing questions of guilt, appropriateness, alternatives, and communal responsibility which divorced persons ask the church. However, such an approach to divorce leads the church not only into some rather inhumane treatment of divorced people, but also puts us on some shaky biblical and theological ground. While divorce is specifically condemned by Jesus in the earliest Gospel (Mark 10:11-12), nowhere does Jesus say that divorce is an unforgivable offense. His words against divorce do not vary greatly in intensity from his words against many other sins. The later Gospels (Matthew 19:4-9, Luke 16:18), while expressly condemning divorce, seem to allow for certain extenuating circumstances. When Paul repeats the command of Jesus on divorce, he adds even more extenuating circumstances (I Corinthians 7:15).

In other words, while divorce is condemned by Jesus, and while the church sought to uphold the strong words of Jesus against divorce, from an early date the church sought to deal with specific persons and their specific circumstances by appealing to certain extenuating conditions when divorce might be permissible.

All of this is to say that, if divorce is not an unforgivable sin, then the church has a strong second option in dealing with it: We can deal with it as creatively, sensitively, corporately, and graciously as we would deal with any other individual or corporate sin. This is the point of view with which divorce is discussed in this chapter.

While the church has always had Christians who sever their marriage bonds, the church has never devised liturgical means for dealing with that severance. Therefore, we have no model, no historical precedent for a liturgy of divorce. This puts us in a rather odd situation since, as we have noted from the beginning of this book, part of the power of liturgy is its sameness, its continuity with what has gone before, its inherently conserving and conservative quality.

But one of the reasons for this book is that, for the first time in a long time, the church is having to think about liturgy in ways in which we have not had to think about it before. We are having to do what the church has done only on rare occasions in its history:

construct new liturgies. On previous occasions when we have had to rethink and reconstruct our worship life, we have had to do so usually because of some fundamental shift in the culture or world in which those liturgies were celebrated.

For instance, the Reformation came about not only because people's theology had changed but also because people's culture had changed. The invention of the printing press, the rise of modern science, economics, language, nation-states, and a host of other factors contributed to the need for a fundamental ordering of our worship life. Many of the old rituals did not work anymore. The church had to be more intentional about its worship, more self-reflective, more conscious of what it was doing and not doing—in order to reform its prayer life to meet new needs of people and new accents of the faith.

In the midst of current social upheaval, changing world orders, shifts in thought and art, new or restored comprehension of the faith, once again the church must be more intentional about how it prays. We must carefully examine what we are doing and what we are not doing when we worship.

In a society where the divorce rate has been skyrocketing for the past decade, where, in some places, there are now as many new divorces as new marriages, the church needs to ask itself what it is doing to care for people who experience this trauma. What is God's word to them? What is God's word to *us?* Out of those questions may arise an attempt to construct a liturgical response to divorce.

Because we have no official or even unofficial liturgy dealing with divorce, we would like to share a trial liturgy of reconciliation related to divorce, a possible model for a liturgy of divorce, an attempt to minister to a specific human need through the liturgy. We suggest that you take the following rite, not as an ideal model, but as an example from which your church might struggle with its own liturgy of divorce.

This liturgy is not our own. It was designed by the Rev. David H. Benson, an Episcopal priest in Missouri, and Ms. Sherrill H. Akyol, a therapist in New York. While there are aspects of this proposed rite which we might have done differently, we offer it as a responsible attempt to address this pressing pastoral need.

Note, in the beginning, that the authors call this a *"Recognition of a Divorce."* This is not a blessing, a celebration, an announcement, or a making of a divorce. Rather, it is an honest recognition by the church that two of its members have severed their marriage bond. It was developed by those who themselves have experienced divorce.

A Service for Recognition of a Divorce

OPENING STATEMENT: (priest)

If anyone is in Christ, he is a new creation; the old has passed away, behold the new has come. All this is from God, who through Christ reconciled us to himself and gave us the ministry of reconciliation. (II Cor. 5:17–18)

Dear Friends: We have come together to recognize before God the death of a marriage. We hold before him the pain, the anger, the guilt, and the loneliness that have been present in that death and ask for his mercy and redemption.

But we are here also to proclaim that death, by the grace of God, is not an end but a beginning of resurrection to new life.

For in the death and resurrection of our Lord Jesus Christ, God has revealed himself to us as one who is able to bring resurrection where there is death, as one who forgives our sins, and calls us to newness of life.

We are witnesses, therefore, to both death and resurrection, to both the sinfulness and forgiveness that are ours who are members one of another in Christ.

But as members one of another we are called to be even more than witnesses. We are called to be a reconciling community within which newness may be nurtured. As we were called upon to nurture and support _____ and _____ in their marriage, we now commit ourselves to nurture and support _____ (and _____) as he/she (they) declare(s) to us the death of that relationship and begin(s) a new life among us.

Let us then confess our sins of the old life, both individual and corporate, to Almighty God; knowing that if we confess our sins, he is faithful and just to forgive them.

CONFESSION OF THE DIVORCED INDIVIDUAL(S):
I confess to Almighty God and to my brothers and sisters in the Body of Christ that I have sinned by my own fault in thought, word, and deed. I have sinned especially against _____ and our child(ren). I acknowledge that my sins have contributed to the death of our marriage, and I pray Almighty God to have mercy on me and forgive me all my sins.

GENERAL CONFESSION OF A SINFUL COMMUNITY:
We here present, on behalf of the community of which _____ and _____ and their child(ren) have been a part, do confess that we have not done all in our power to uphold and support them in their marriage. We have often been indifferent and blind to their needs and mistaken our needs for theirs, and we pray Almighty God to have mercy on us and forgive us our sins.

ABSOLUTION:
Almighty God have mercy on you, forgive you all your sins through our Lord Jesus Christ, strengthen you in all goodness, and by the power of the Holy Spirit keep you in eternal life. Amen.

SCRIPTURE READINGS:
Old Testament Lessons: Isaiah 43:18–21 (25)
Micah 4:6b–7
Hosea 11:8–11a
Psalm: 103 or 116
Gospels: Matthew 7:7–11
Matthew 5:3–10
John 15:1–5

THE HOMILY

DECLARATIONS:
(Questions asked by the priest)

_____ (and _____), do you now declare before us here assembled that you no longer live in a state of holy matrimony?

A. I (We) do declare it.
Do you, _____, freely forgive those sins committed against you by _____ in that former marriage?

A. I do forgive them by God's help.
(Repeat this question and answer of the other person, if both be participating.)
Will you continue a concern for _____ as a child of God and a brother (sister) in Christ?

A. I will by God's help.

[Option #1, replacing the above question and answer:

And do you renounce absolutely any bond between you in mind, body and spirit from this day forward, continuing only a concern for _____ as a child of God and a brother (sister) in Christ?

A. I do will it and ask God's help.

Will you share mutual responsibility with _____ for the welfare of your child(ren), realizing that the parent-child relationship is not broken?

A. That is my intention and to that end I seek God's help.]

[Option #2, to be added to the foregoing questions and answers. Priest questions the congregation:

Will all of you witnessing these declarations release this person/these persons from his/her (their) promises to you and will you release marital expectation of her/him (them)?

A. We release you from those promises made before God and the community in your marriage vows that we may uphold you as (a) single person(s) beloved by God.]

PRAYERS:
In peace then let us pray to the Lord:

For the peace and unity of the Church of God, that it may be filled with truth and love, and be found without fault at the day of your coming, O Christ,
Hear us, Lord.

For _____ and _____, who have suffered the death of their marriage, that they may accept your newness and be blessed with your peace and freedom.
Hear us, Lord.

For their child(ren) and that he/she (they) may continue to know the love of the parents and above all know the love of a heavenly Father. May she/he (they) share in your newness.
Hear us, Lord.

For those people, some present and some absent, who have strengthened and supported this marriage in the past, and now undertake to support new life.
Hear us, Lord.

For those who are not now reconciled to this separation, we ask your healing and peace.
Hear us, Lord.

That in all anxieties for our future we may continue steadfastly to put our trust in you.
Hear us, Lord.

For the grace to assume new responsibilities, that we may serve you in others and love them as you love us.
Hear us, Lord.

In the communion of saints let us commend ourselves and one another to Christ our God.
We commend ourselves to you, O Lord.

THE COLLECT:
O Lord our God, accept the fervent prayers of your people; in the multitude of your mercies look with compassion upon us and all who turn to you for help; for you are gracious, O lover of souls, and to you we give glory, praise and thanks, Father, Son and Holy Spirit, now and forever. *Amen.*

THE RECOGNITION AND AFFIRMATION:
(Priest and Congregation)

_____ (and _____), on behalf of the church which blessed your marriage, we now recognize the end of that marriage. We affirm you as (a) single person(s) among us and we pledge you our support as you continue to seek God's help and guidance for the new life which you have undertaken in faith.

THE PEACE:
The peace of the Lord be always with you.
And also with you.

(OFFERTORY, if Eucharist is to follow)

EUCHARIST

THE BLESSING:
The blessing of God the Father, God the Son and God the Holy
Spirit be with you this day and always.

THE DISMISSAL:
.Let us go forth into the world, rejoicing in the power of the spirit.

THE RESPONSE:
Thanks be to God.

Catechesis and Divorce
Few pastoral or catechetical issues have been avoided as much as divorce. Marriages sometimes die, but the Christian partners and their
children survive. If we care for persons and desire to minister to
their needs, we will need a catechesis for divorce. We are not, of
course, recommending a program of catechesis which encourages
divorce. But we are recommending a program of catechesis that
will help the whole church, children, youth, and adults, to understand the theological and moral, the psychological and social issues
related to divorce so that the church might better minister to those
persons and families in which there has been a divorce or one is
contemplated.

Catechesis Within the Divorce Ritual
Previously we discussed the need for a divorce ritual that reconciles
those who have broken this marriage covenant and reincorporates
them within a Christian community where healing and growth
might occur. Since such a ritual does not as yet exist it is difficult to
propose catechetical norms. Nevertheless if such a ritual is to

emerge we need to consider the catechetical elements which might be present. In that regard we suggest texts which focus on God's promise of forgiveness and healing of estrangement. Such as: Isaiah 43:18-21, 25; Micah 4:6b-7, Hosea 11:8-11a; Psalms 103 and 116; Matthew 5:3-10; Matthew 7:7-10 and John 15:1-5. Homilies on such texts would be important catechetical elements within a divorce ritual.

Catechesis for Divorce

Typically, almost every married couple, at some point in their lives, find their marriage in difficulty. For some these difficulties become so serious that they enter a period of separation with the possibility of reunion at a later date. Still others make the difficult and painful decision to break their marriage covenant and go through a difficult period of waiting before a divorce is finalized.

In all three of these cases counseling is called for and indeed essential. The persons involved will need help to deal with their hurt, anger, guilt and other emotions. Some marriages will be healed and desire to reaffirm their marriage covenant; others will end in estrangement. In any case, catechesis, along with counseling, can play a significant role. Importantly, catechesis will need to be considered not only for the couple but also for their children, closest friends, and others affected by their struggles.

First, catechesis must focus on reconciliation and the healing of brokenness. Second, it needs to help persons discover their own worth as a child of God. Third, it needs to help them discover the special learnings and graces which this difficult period makes possible. Fourth, they need help to focus on their personal spiritual journey and to discern where God is leading them. Last, they need to be helped to grow in their devotional life. At few times in their lives will they need more the resources of prayer and meditation.

Most divorce catechesis needs to provide opportunities for divorced persons and for the children of divorced parents to deal with their particular needs in the light of the Gospel.

Rubrics for Recognition of a Divorce

Liturgically speaking, the closest relative of the experimental "Liturgy for Recognition of a Divorce" is the church's rites of reconciliation of a penitent. While this particular experimental rite speaks of divorce in terms of death and grief over a dead marriage, we personally prefer a rite which is more explicitly concerned to make a bold, either private or public, statement of the presence of sin and an equally bold statement of the availability of grace. In one sense we therefore might look on this service as *a special adaptation of the service for the reconciliation of the penitent.* (See Chapter 13) The justification for a public recognition of divorce is that, in divorce, we are dealing with a peculiar situation where many people's thoughts, commitments, children, parents, feelings, and relationships are involved. Marriage was a public declaration of commitment along with public assumptions of responsibility for the commitment. Therefore, recognition of divorce must somehow involve a more-or-less public recognition of the termination of that commitment. We all have a stake in the forming of a marriage or the dissolution of a marriage.

Pastoral discretion must be exercised in deciding what form our liturgical response to divorce might take. We walk a theological and pastoral tightrope in our dealings with divorced and divorcing persons. On the one hand, we want to be honest and truthful about the church's values in regard to marriage and its covenant. On the other, we want to be compassionate and evangelistic about the church's care and grace for those who, for whatever reasons, are unable to keep the marriage covenant.

These foregoing thoughts on recognition of divorce are offered in an attempt to invite congregations to think about the problem rather than avoid it, assuming that, in the church's care of people in crisis, some things are *not* better when they are left unsaid. At time of divorce, our task is to speak the truth in love, true to our Gospel and its law, which is, itself, love.

·9·

Thanksgiving for the Birth or Adoption of a Child

Of all God's gifts which are bestowed in this life, few gifts equal God's gift of a child. The Gospel stories begin with a child, a holy child which will be a sign of God's grace and presence. Not only the baby Jesus, but every baby is a sign of divine grace and presence—God with us in the flesh.

And yet, few blessings in life are as great a burden as the gift of a child. Children demand patience, time, courage, wisdom, and trustworthiness from us. At the "Thanksgiving for the Birth or Adoption of a Child," the church joins a child's parents in praising God for the gift of a child and asking God's grace in our nurture and care of this child.

This ritual is important as a public time to celebrate the advent of new life into our midst. It signifies a married couple's movement into the vocation of parenthood as well as the church's commitment not only to care for and support the new child but also the church's commitment to care for and support the new parents.

If we are to take parental preparation for child baptism seriously, as we advocated in Chapter 1, "Thanksgiving for the Birth or Adoption of a Child" provides the church an excellent opportunity to begin discussion with the parents about the content and form of their pre-baptismal catechesis. By publicly giving thanks when a child is born or adopted, we also make it easier for parents to postpone Christian initiation of their child until pre-baptismal catechesis is completed.

When a child is adopted, the thanksgiving for the child can be even more important. In adoption, because there generally has not been a long period of pregnancy and preparation, the parents and the community need an opportunity to publicly affirm this child, to claim the child as part of the household of faith. Sometimes an adopted child may have already been baptized, in which cases the thanksgiving is doubly important.

The 1979 *Book of Common Prayer* has a "Thanksgiving for the Birth or Adoption of a Child." Its form is as follows:

1. *Address:* A statement of the occasion of the Thanksgiving, using the Christian names of the parents, brothers and sisters of the new child, and the child.

2. *Thanksgiving:* The Magnificat (Song of Mary), Psalm 116, Psalm 23 or other suitable acts of Thanksgiving may be read responsively.

3. *Prayers and Blessing:* Prayers for the new child and its parents and family. Prayers for the church in its care of the child, a blessing pronounced before the family. During the prayers, members of the family may wish to express, in their own words, their own thanks for the child.

4. *Peace:* An opportunity for friends and family to exchange the peace with the family.

As usual, the form and content of the service may be adapted to suit the specific context of and participants in the service.

Catechesis and Parenthood

Catechesis for Christian parenthood is almost unknown. We operate as if anyone can become a good parent and as if child rearing is natural. Not so, especially in a day of changing roles of men and women. For example, while there is nothing abnormal about men rearing children, men will need particular help to play this role, for they have so few role models to emulate. Catechesis for child rearing after the birth or adoption of children is not too late, but it surely would be helpful if we prepared earlier.

The divisions of labor between men and women will continue to shift. While women have traditionally cared for children, men can and will desire to acquire the same skills. We need to develop parenthood catechesis for both men and women, beginning with youth. The duties of Christian parents, and the developmental and spiritual needs of children need to be explored. If the procreation and nurturing of children are two of the implications of Christian marriage, we will need to help persons understand parenting before they make a decision on marriage. Since children are entrusted to the whole congregation, and all Christians share responsibility for children's Christian nurture, catechesis for child rearing will need to be provided for all members of the community of faith.

Catechesis for Parenthood

The period before an adoption is finalized or during pregnancy is an opportune time for catechesis. Persons often go to classes, for nine months, to prepare to meet the physical needs of children. Is it too much to expect that couples do the same to prepare to meet the spiritual needs of children? Further, other children in a family also need to be prepared for the presence of an addition to their family.

It has been our contention that we celebrate the birth or adoption of a child shortly after birth or adoption and that as of that date a baptismal catechesis begin to prepare parents for their child's baptism which would therefore take place within the first year of its life. In this case, however, we are recommending additional catechesis prior to this first liturgy of welcome and before baptismal catechesis.

Catechesis in this case needs to focus on the parents' spiritual health and be seen as an opportunity for them to deepen their own devotional life. It is also a time to consider the naming of their child as few issues are more important than naming. For example, what biblical person or saint might we choose as a companion and friend and role model for our child? Further, whom might we choose as our child's godparents? To whom would we want to entrust our child's Christian nurture if anything were to happen to us? During this period we might help parents learn the skills of storytelling and singing as well as help them to gather resources to help them communicate their faith to our children during their first years.

Rubrics for the Thanksgiving on the Birth or Adoption of a Child

The rite of Thanksgiving should occur as soon as possible after the birth of a child or after receiving a child by adoption. The rite should occur in a usual Sunday service, normally before the peace at the Eucharist. The parents and family should stand in some prominent place in front of the congregation. A brief form of the service may be used at the hospital or home. If this is done, it is best to at least have some designated representative of the entire congregation present at the service.

During the service opportunity should be given for parents and other members of the family to express thanks for the child in their own words. Some mention should be made, in the service, of the future baptism of the child and the pre-baptismal catechesis which begins at this time.

· 10 ·

Moving and the Blessing
of a New Home

We are a people on the move, a pilgrim people, exiles. Statistics show that the average American family moves every 3.2 years. People move to pursue and advance their careers, or when they sell their home and move into a nursing home, or when they divorce, or when a partner in a marriage dies, or when they leave home for college, or a host of other dislocations.

Movement from one place requires saying good-by to familiar friends and faces, accustomed places, old patterns of life. Moving can be like death. In fact, in recent interviews with middle-aged married couples, moving was rated as the second most stressful experience the couples encountered, second only to the death of a close friend or relative. Moving also carries with it the possibility of new life, new friends and faces, new life patterns which, because of the upheaval of moving, can be changed for the better. Moving can be like rebirth.

A Ritual for Moving

It is our contention that churches must give closer attention to how they help people move, how they say hello and good-by to members of the congregation. There was a time in our past when the average Christian was born, baptized, nurtured, married, lived and was buried in the same church. In such a time of stability, the community did not need to think about some things which we must think about now. This is why the past has not given us official, detailed rituals for moving from one place to another, and only a few, rarely used rituals for the blessing of a new home.

The model of a ritual of moving would be a typical rite of passage, such as the ones discussed in earlier chapters. We are addressing the human crisis which is precipitated by the movement from one place to another. A good rite of moving must therefore have opportunities for separation, transition, and incorporation. In envisioning what such a rite might look like, we think it would normally have the following parts:

- *A Declaration:* who the persons are who are making the move and a statement of why they are making the move.
- *Remembrance:* the past which has been shared, something from the store of memories of this place and its experiences, an opportunity to claim what this place and its people have meant to the people in this place.
- *Proclamation:* Scripture along with a short meditation or homily on the biblical-theological significance of this move. Some reflection upon what it means to say good-by or hello as Christians, a reflection upon what it means to be people on the move.
- *Response:* an opportunity for people to respond to what the proclaimed word means to them at this time of moving, a public word of farewell.
- *Blessing and Sending Forth:* The community bestows God's blessing upon the participants, particularly upon those who are now moving to another place. In a way, this is the core of the liturgy of moving. A blessing is an age-old way of committing someone to God's love and care, even though that person is physically separated from us. "God be with you as you leave us" is the essence of its intent.

The specific format and content of this service of moving would depend upon the circumstances of the move and the participants. Ideally, such a service should occur within the congregation's morning worship service where the service can be done with the presence and support of the whole community, giving the whole community opportunity to participate. A farewell Eucharist would then be celebrated with the blessing and sending forth ending the service.

Blessing of a New Home

In the earliest days of the church, the church found it helpful to bless or consecrate places and buildings. Pagan customs included the sanctifying of homes and the adoption of household gods for the protection and blessing of homes. Our homes are where we have our primary and most formative experiences of God and God's love through the family. Our homes represent places of comfort, safety, relaxation, sanctuary, growth, mutual dependence, and self-giving. Perhaps that was why the Puritans referred to the family and its home as a "little church," or a "church within the church."

Those of us who have moved from one house to another know that we are doing much more than merely changing our addresses where we change houses. We are moving to an entirely new context for a family's life together. This move can be especially traumatic if the move to a new home has occurred as the result of a death in the family, or poor health which requires moving to a nursing home, or a divorce. By blessing the new home, claiming it as a new place for family life and the presence of God, the church can help the family or person make this transition a time of renewal and rebirth rather than simply a painful severing of the past.

The service for the "Celebration for a Home" (p. 131 ff., *The Book of Occasional Services,* The Church Hymnal Corporation, 1979) is a fine service for the blessing of a home. Generally, a service for the blessing of a new home should contain a statement of purpose for gathering in the home, appropriate Scripture (for example, Genesis 18:1-8, 3 John 1-6a, 11, 13-15, John 11:5; 12:1-3), the Eucharist, and various prayers which may be said in various rooms of the house for the various forms of family life which will take place in the rooms. The service can conclude with a final blessing followed by a meal or reception for guests.

We do not so much bless houses as we bless the home which is formed within the house. In blessing a home, we are publicly claiming this place as a place of God, a holy endeavor with important spiritual consequences for those who live there. We are invoking the presence of God into the midst of our mundane and everyday life together.

Catechesis, Moving and the Blessing of Homes

While moving has become a way of life for many, it has a disruptive power upon our lives. Even when a geographical move is considered desirable, it causes anxiety. Similarly, moving into a new home can cause surprising feelings of dis-ease. Christians may be called to be a pilgrim people, but there is something in us that gets attached to places and buildings. In order that meaningful rituals for moving can be developed, catechesis on moving, its theological meaning and psychological effects will need to be explored and discussed. Further, while rituals do exist for the blessing of a new home, as well as blessings of all homes on Epiphany and Easter, few persons are aware of these rites and their content. It is essential that catechesis address their needs for awareness and understanding.

Catechesis and Moving—the Blessing of Homes

Catechesis in preparation for a geographical move or a move into a new home should explore a particular person or family's needs in terms of their beliefs, attitudes and behaviors. Assistance will be needed to help parents aid their children deal with their move. It is also a time to aid families in their spiritual life.

Preparation for a move is a good time for persons to reflect upon their spiritual life and to discern that to which God is calling them. Catechesis can help persons better understand their vocation of life in the spirit and the ministries to which God is calling them in their new context. It is a time for the examination of consciousness, for an awareness of God's grace in their lives and for spiritual transformations.

Preparation for a move is also a good time for persons to reflect upon their life in the church. Catechesis can help families better understand the mission and ministry of the church, their calling in the church and the sort of faith community they need to nurture them in the next stage of their pilgrimage. In this regard, catechesis can assist families to investigate possible parishes before they move so that they can avoid looking for a church and be provided with a sense of stability at the beginning of their move.

Catechesis can at this time help persons and families to reflect on this spiritual life in the home. It can help them to develop a more meaningful devotional life. Further, it can help them consider new home symbols and works of art that will help them express, enhance, and enliven their faith.

Rubrics for Moving

Each church should carefully examine how it welcomes new members into its midst. It is not enough to simply transfer a person's church membership from one place to another. In congregations where the membership is fairly transient, and mobility is high, a continuous program of catechesis and integration of new persons into congregational life is essential.

People must be prepared for movement into a new congregation by being given the necessary information and support which will enable them to be full and functioning members. Congregational membership instruction, sponsors, get-acquainted dinners, neighborhood groups may help here.

Likewise, we must take care, in saying good-by to people, so that we may publicly recognize what they have meant to our church's life as well as do what we can to smooth their transition to a new place. A short service of prayer on moving day, a special ritual of leaving in the worship service on the last Sunday before they move, letters of introduction to a church in the town where they are moving can be ways of caring for people who move. If a letter of introduction is sent to another church, it could mention what tasks the persons performed in their old congregation and indicate what gifts and talents they exercised in that church. The letter could then be read in a ritual of reception into the new congregation.

Rubrics for the Blessing of a Home

The blessing of a home should be a time for the church to join a family in celebrating their new home as well as setting this home apart as a place of God's presence. We could also imagine blessing the room of a nursing home patient, or any other place where a person lives.

The liturgy may begin in the living room of the home, or on the steps before the front door. Then the worshippers move into each room of the house, praying for God's blessing upon the various family functions which will occur in that room. As the congregation moves from one room to the next, candles may be lit in each room to signify the presence of God in this place. Be sure to include the family children in each part of the liturgy. A Eucharist could then be celebrated in the dining room or living room of the home, having family members assist the celebrant in the prayers and in the distribution of the elements.

Throughout this liturgy, we are reminding ourselves that God meets us in the midst of the mundane, redeems the ordinary days, and makes holy the places where we go about our lives.

· 11 ·

Ordination and Celebration
of a New Ministry

I
n Chapter 1 we affirmed that all Christians share in Christ's ministry to the world by virtue of their baptism. Baptism is the fundamental "ordaining" sacrament which gives us the gifts and the
mandate to share in Christ's mission of bringing the world to God.

But, from its beginning, the body of Christ found it helpful to
recognize and designate some of its members to lead the church in
its ministry, to edify and oversee the community, to focus the community's attention on our shared symbols and mission, and to preside in the community's worship. These leaders were seen as God's
gift to the church, a gracious gift of a loving God who did not
leave his people without leadership.

In the New Testament period, leadership within the church appears to have been multifarious and diverse. Our *bishops* ("over-
seers"), *deacons* ("servants" "stewards"), and *presbyters* ("elders,"
"priests") are mentioned. But there are apostles, teachers, healers,
and prophets as well (see I Cor. 12:28-30). While the church recognized a variety of gifts which it found edifying for a variety of
needs, two basic ministerial functions underlie this variety: service
and oversight, *diakonia* and *episcope*. It appears that "deacons" assisted the bishop in oversight of a particular congregation (until
the third century, bishops generally exercised oversight of only
one congregation) and cared for the needs of the congregation's
widows, orphans, and poor. "Bishops" led congregational catechesis, preached, and presided in the congregation's worship.

A third order of ministry emerged during this period, "elders." At first, elders seem to have functioned as a congregational governing body, much the same way as elders functioned in Jewish synagogues. They elected a bishop for the congregation and decided in congregational disputes. By the end of the third century, bishops began to oversee a number of congregations, and individual elders were placed in charge of one congregation, functioning in much the same way as the bishops functioned earlier. The elders were seen as the bishop's representative within a congregation. This arrangement eventually led to the hierarchical priesthood arrangement which became the distinguishing feature of the ordained ministry in the Middle Ages. Gradually, the elder was known as "priest," the basic, ordained leader of a congregation, the one whose office combined the roles of oversight and service.

Ordained Christians, i.e. *priests,* are thus a function of the shared priesthood of all Christians. Their chief function within the congregation is edification of the congregation through teaching (catechesis), preaching, discipline, guidance, care, administration of the sacraments, and a symbolic representation of the servanthood of Christ within the congregation; that is, to be a spiritual resource. In edifying the community, priests must not take other Christians' ministry away from them, or allow them to give their ministry to their priests. The role of the priest is to illumine, equip, support, confirm, serve, and symbolize the ministry of all his or her fellow Christians, not to take their ministry upon his or her shoulders.

Liturgically speaking, the purpose of the ordination rite is for the designation of symbol-bearers or leaders for the church. The ordained ministry is merely a function of the church, necessary only because of the church's need to have someone bear and illumine its symbols of identity so that it may be about its God-given business. In ordination, the community bestows its blessing upon the ordinand, recognizes God's call of this person to the priesthood or pastoral ministry, and prays for God's gifts to enable this person to fulfill the designated function of priest.

It is not that other people could not pray, preach, teach, heal, and administer sacraments as well as or better than the priest. It is that, when the priest does these things, he or she functions as the symbol-bearer for the community, under orders from the community, as the officially recognized, corporately designated person to bear and interpret the community's shared symbols. And that makes all the difference. Priests appear necessary to illumine the "priest" in all of us.

Historically, ordination consists of the action of laying-on-of-hands and prayer. The laying-on-of-hands is an ancient gesture of blessing, a bestowal of power and authority. It is a vivid, sacramental reminder that a priest's authority comes, not from his or her own will to be a priest, not even from his or her superior training or noble personal attributes. A priest's authority arises from God's church.

No one can be a priest by private desire to be one. The community expects the person to be able to testify to a personal vocation from God to the priesthood, but the community also reserves the right to confirm or reject that call. The call is from God *and* God's church. The laying-on-of-hands signifies the church's authorization and blessing of one's vocation to the ordained ministry. In some churches, a bishop presides at the service of ordination, assisted by other priests. Non-episcopal churches ordain through a group of elders or priests who lay hands upon the ordinand. The presence and action of the priests and/or bishop signifies the continuity of the church's ordained ministry with the apostolic ministries of the past. It also signifies the new priest's reception into the membership of the presbyterate or priesthood, not as a superior status, but as a collegial, shared burden which is bestowed by the church.

The prayer which is joined to the laying-on-of-hands is generally an invocation for the gifts and graces which the new priest will need for the care and nurture of the flock. In so praying, the church recognizes that, ultimately, ministry and the skills and charism it requires are gifts of God for the edification and preservation of his church.

Normatively speaking, the core of all rites of ordination is the public laying-on-of-hands (by someone who is already a priest) and prayer (invoking the Spirit's presence and gifts for this person in the exercise of his or her ministry). The presence and active participation of the church is necessary as a sign that the ordained ministry arises out of, must be confirmed by, and exists for the shared ministry of all Christians. Finally, no one can become a priest without authorization by the church, for the ordained ministry is a function of the church. Outside the authorization of the church, ordination has no meaning. The "twofold call"—from God *and* the church—is the essential prerequisite for ordination.

Celebration of a New Ministry

When a congregation receives a new priest, this new pastoral relationship offers a wonderful opportunity to celebrate not only the installation of a new spiritual resource and pastoral leader but also an occasion to affirm the shared ministry of all Christians to one another. The induction must in no way be seen as a congregational re-ordination of the priest, rather it is a time for the recognition of a new ministry as well as recognition of the mutual dependency of priest and people upon each other's ministries for the fulfillment of the total ministry of Christ through the church.

The service should normally be conducted by a bishop, district superintendent, president or some other official who is responsible for sending and/or approving this new pastoral appointment.

The service should have the following parts:

• *Declaration* of the purpose of the service and naming of the officiant and the person to be inducted.

• *Proclamation* through scripture, prayer, hymn and anthem of the word at this time of induction. The lessons should focus on the nature of Christian ministry. Some appropriate lessons are: Joshua 1:7-9, Psalm 43, Romans 12:1-18 or Ephesians 4:7, 11-16, and John 15:9-16 or Luke 10:1-2.

• *Response* to the word from the congregation in the form of greetings, declarations of intent, signs of support, special hymns or anthems.

• *Induction* of the new pastor through the presentation of various symbols of the new pastor's duties. These symbols (Bible, a vessel of water, stole, prayer book, oil, keys to the church, bread and wine, etc.) should be presented by various members of the congregation, young and old, each with a short statement of its purpose. These symbols, presented by the congregation, become symbolic reminders that the duties and gifts of the pastoral ministry arise out of the shared ministry of the congregation.

• *Eucharist,* at which time the service is concluded, with the newly installed priest presiding for the first time.

• *Blessing* by the visiting official or the new pastor at the end of the service.

Catechesis and Ordination

For too long we have perpetuated the idea of professional ministers and neglected the common ministry all Christians share by their baptism. Correspondingly we have ignored the nature and function of priesthood as one ministry in the church. Catechesis needs to help people understand that priests are the authorized bearers and interpreters of the community's symbols, identified and called by God and the community to illumine the priest in all of us. The clergy are sacramental persons whose unique role is to "bring God to people" and not to perform all the ministries assigned to the church. All baptized Christians should understand their calling to minister, to be equipped for these ministries, to identify and encourage some of their number to assume the ministry of priesthood, and to aid their priests in developing this ministry and their shared ministry.

EXAMPLE:

A parish party on the anniversary of their pastor's ordination could focus upon a celebration of the congregation's many ministries with opportunities to enlist children, youth, and adults in these and new ministries. A special group of those who are considering church vocations could be organized at this time.

Catechesis Within the Rite of Ordination
In order that this rite can assume its full significance, we need to emphasize the catechetical function of the sermon at this important event, as well as the importance of the charge to the new priest and to the people. Catechetically, it is also essential that the laity as well as the clergy play a significant role in the ceremony, thereby establishing both their joint and particular ministries.

EXAMPLE:

The children in a parish might make some gift to be presented at the ordination; for example, a white chasuble and stoles with all their handprints in various colors could be made. Following the laying-on-of-hands by the clergy, the children could vest their new priest.

Catechesis for the Rite of Ordination
or Celebration of a New Ministry
Ordinations are major events in the life of a congregation. We typically neglect the possibility of catechesis or ministry for children, youth, and adults at such times. Children, youth, and adults can help to prepare for and participate in the liturgy. It is conceivable that the day of an ordination could be used for catechesis.

EXAMPLE:

Following a simple luncheon, the bishop and future priest could depart for retreat in the chapel or other room. All ages can learn the hymns and make other preparations for participation in the ordination liturgy. Films, art, activities, and discussions on the meaning of ordination can be held in intergenerational groups or in learning centers.

Rubrics for Ordination

While churches may differ on what type of ordained persons are to lay hands upon a recipient of ordination (bishop, bishop with priests, priests only), nothing in the rite should obscure the central action of laying-on-of-hands with prayer. Fortunately, new liturgies for ordination are simplified so that the central action of ordination is clearer than it was in some older rites.

The rite should be a full service of corporate worship including a sermon (preferably on the ministry) and concluding with the Eucharist at which the new priest presides.

The service should begin with the presentation of the candidate by a representative layperson along with some brief statement by the layperson concerning the congregation's acclamation of the candidate.

It is fitting to invite a number of clergy to participate in the service and the laying-on-of-hands as a gesture of the shared and collegial nature of ordained ministry.

In celebrating the creation of a new priest for God's church, the church is again reminded of its shared priesthood among all the baptized. Our mutual ministry is again called to mind and focused upon, symbolized afresh in this new priest. As the bishop says to the new priest in the Service of Ordination in the *Book of Common Prayer:*

> the Church is the family of God, the body of Christ, and the temple of the Holy Spirit. All baptized people are called to make Christ known as Savior and Lord, and to share in the renewing of his world. Now you are called to work as a pastor, priest, and teacher ... As a priest, it will be your task to proclaim by word and deed the Gospel of Jesus Christ, and to fashion your life in accordance with its precepts. You are to love and serve the people among whom you work, caring alike for young and old, strong and weak, rich and poor. You are to preach, to declare God's forgiveness to penitent sinners, to pronounce God's blessing, to share in the administration of Holy Baptism and in the celebration of the mysteries of Christ's Body and Blood, and to perform the other ministrations entrusted to you. In all that you do, you are to nourish Christ's people from the riches of his grace, and to strengthen them to glorify God in this life and in the life to come.

·12·

Retirement

In Japan, when a man reaches his sixty-first birthday, his family gives him a party. He dresses in a red kimono and makes merry, often engaging in silly, childlike jokes and antics. At about the same age, the Japanese grandmother hands over her pots, pans, and other cooking utensils to the younger women of the household and goes on a holiday. For both older men and older women, these rituals represent the passage into retirement, the joyful release from the burdens and cares of work.

It is also customary for Japanese elders to celebrate their eightieth birthday by doing something strenuous or creative such as taking a long trip or climbing a mountain. In so doing, they signify that the last years of life are years of transition, growth, and continuing self-worth.

Unfortunately, our Western culture has a different view of aging and retirement. People in our society are not proud to be old. Retirement often brings feelings of being "over the hill," of little use, incompetent, and without worth.

These negative associations of retirement are especially troubling in a time when our country has an increasingly larger proportion of older people. What can the church do, liturgically and catechetically, to minister to people during the life crisis of aging and retirement?

The goals of a liturgical response to retirement would be to help aging persons interpret this life passage in the light of the Gospel, to prepare them for the challenges and opportunities of retirement, and to recognize these persons as persons of value and continuing importance whose lives and ministry are continuing rather than ending. Unfortunately, the closest thing we have to a ritual for retirement is the "retirement banquet" which is often a rather faltering, pitiful attempt to recognize this important milestone in a person's life; it usually makes the recipient of the honor feel that he or she is being "put out to pasture" with a gold watch and a letter of thanks from the company president. For women who spend their working lives as housewives and mothers, we do not even have as feeble a response as a banquet and a gold watch.

We must see aging and retirement not as a terminal phase in human development but as continuing the process of development. Research shows that personal adaptation to aging depends upon a person's self-perception and interpretation of him or herself in the aging process. We have little to fear from aging—as long as we keep growing.

However, in our ministry to aging persons, a number of factors complicate our task. People retire earlier now. A retired person may still be in excellent health and may still expect many more years of life. Our urban, mobile society tends to cut older people off from their families, giving them too little opportunity to contribute to the life of a family and giving the family too little chance to support and be with older people. Many of our elderly are isolated, living alone. Related to this factor is the rise of professional care for the incapacitated elderly and institutionalization—which can be lonely and degrading. Modern life has seen a decline in the status of our elders. In another day, our elders were teachers and guardians of the young, sources of wisdom and experience. In a rapidly changing, technological world, the old seem to have few skills or little knowledge which new generations can utilize. Thus, our old are made to feel like, and are treated like, burdens.

Any liturgical response to retirement must be part of a larger counseling and educational program for older people in the church. It must be a true rite of passage, designed to speak to the needed separations, transitions, and new incorporations which a retiring person must make. It may be done in a service of congregational worship, although it must be more than a mere "old folks appreciation day." It may be a quiet ritual for the home or be a reception into a retired person's class or support group within the church.

In a ritual for retirement, we could envisage the following parts:

• *A Declaration* of the purpose of the rite; i.e., to recognize the retirement of someone from his or her job and to help begin a new life as a person who, now free from those demands and responsibilities, may begin a new ministry.

• *Remembrance* of the job which is terminating; recollection, reminiscence, testimonials.

• *Proclamation* through Scripture and homily of the beauty of a long and productive life, the joy of rest and recreation, the satisfaction of a job well done, an affirmation of our vocation as Christians rather than simply holders of a job, and encouragement for the fresh beginning which is now being made.

• *Response* by the retiring person or family and friends to the proclamation.

• *Blessing and Sending Forth.*

Catechesis and Retirement

One of the most significant, difficult, often unwanted and yet typically ignored passages in human life is retirement from the work force. Catechesis can help to prepare persons for meaningful changes in their lives. It must help persons understand the feelings that will accompany retirement and to consider the alternative life choices and life-styles which are now possible. A catechesis of retirement needs to help persons understand vocation as spiritual pilgrimage instead of work, and ministry as to context for serving God and neighbors rather than employment. It can further help persons to understand the process of aging and the ongoing development of their spiritual life.

Until this fundamental catechesis on retirement is done, it will be difficult to develop meaningful rituals for retirement.

In preparation for retirement it is important that we aid all those affected by a retirement with attention to the family and mates of retirees. Everyone in a community needs to consider and prepare for the changes retirement will make in their lives. Even more important will be a catechesis that aids all involved to discern where God is now calling them and what new ministry they will need to prepare for. Catechesis for retirement could also rightfully prepare them for these new ministries.

Rubrics for a Retirement Rite

One important element in a rite of retirement will be the reading of and commentary on Holy Scripture. Readings will need to be chosen with care. Possibilities are Ecclesiastes 3:1-8 on the meaning of time, 1st Corinthians 12:1-11 on the gifts of the spirit and John 3:1-8 on new birth in old age.

Symbolic gifts or acts in the ritual also serve a catechetical purpose. Perhaps a reminder of baptism, the gift of a red garment symbolic of the royal role of a child of the spirit, and an anointing of eyes to see the past afresh and envision the future, of the ears to hear the call of God, and lips so as to speak wisdom in the community. The commitment to a new ministry, accompanied by the sign of the cross, would be an appropriate way to end the rite.

·13·

Reconciliation of the Penitent

Forgiveness of sins is inseparable from the Gospel. The good news which Christ brings is the news of freedom or liberation from all that dehumanizes, alienates, oppresses or limits human social and individual fulfillment—the news of reconciliation or the unity of self, neighbor, God, and creation, the healing of brokenness and the perfection of humanity and creation.

Sin denies this message and is multi-dimensional. *Cosmic sin,* personified in Satan, refers to all those spiritual forces that rebel against God's grace. *Social sin* refers to the political, social, and economic structures we humans create which oppress, corrupt, and destroy creation and the creatures of God. *Personal sin* refers to those internal dispositions and acts which draw us away from love of God and neighbor.

Sin is unnatural. We are aware of sin because our natural state is to be in grace. It may be understandable that we humans live in sin, but it is God's will that we live otherwise. God has created us in his image. We are free to make decisions and to act morally. We are capable of living in our natural, healthy state, or in an unnatural, sinful state. Historically, humanity in its freedom has demonstrated a strange inclination to choose that which is unnatural. God came in Jesus Christ to overwhelm the cosmic powers of evil and establish God's rule or kingdom, to provide us with a sign of new age and a vision of salvation. It is now possible for us to live as we were created to live. There are no more excuses. Our complete freedom has been restored. We are whole, healthy people who can live in community, and for the justice, freedom, equity, unity, and the well-being of all humanity. We are called to live by faith, to see things as they really are, to perceive reality as fulfilled, and to enter upon a journey toward our own and creation's fulfillment. That is, to actualize that which is already our essential condition. To do so, we need to renounce all sin, to turn to Jesus Christ and accept him as the one who has saved us, to put our trust in his grace and to follow his way.

God has made us into new people, whole people, saved people. God's grace makes it possible for us to orient and reorient our spirits toward salvation and thereby actualize our true or natural condition. Still, life provides us with occasions to choose either sin or grace. Sex, alcohol, wealth, and the like are each occasions for sin, but each is also an occasion for grace. God gives us the gift of creation, of history, of opportunity; we can either enhance or distort the goodness God gives and desires.

We all share the human need to face ourselves, to discard our masks and pretenses, and to talk openly to another human being. The church needs to create an atmosphere where we can be ourselves, acknowledge our human condition, and discuss with fellow human beings where we fall short of our true humanity, without being condemned, maligned, or labeled. We need a community where we are accepted as we are, and loved for nothing. We need a community that treats us as redeemed human beings, a community that mirrors for us our saved condition, a community that permits us to share our awareness of sin and offers us free grace in return. In other words, we need a community that makes it possible for us to forgive ourselves. Or better, we need a community that accepts our human existential condition but treats us according to our essential human condition.

The early church was a community that took seriously its call to be a sign of God's rule; it therefore attempted to create a perfect society. As such, it took sin with great seriousness. Persons became Christians at baptism by renouncing sin and its power, by accepting forgiveness for past sin and by committing themselves to live in God's free grace. Sinful acts following baptism were considered unforgivable. However, history did not come to an end (as expected), and the negative implications of this early perfectionism brought the church to a new resolve. Sin was still taken seriously and personal sin was still seen as a concern of the whole church. Indeed, sinful acts after baptism were considered to seriously endanger and disrupt the community. One such sinful action was now permitted, but it resulted in the person being separated from the community (excommunicated) until he/she completed a rigorous program of public confession and penance before being granted forgiveness and reincorporated into the community.

For example, by the ninth century, on the Wednesday before Lent (later to be called Ash Wednesday), the imposition of ashes and several penitential psalms formed a rite of expulsion for those who committed acts of sin. All penitents were thereby excommunicated and placed under discipline during Lent. On Maundy Thursday they participated in a rite of reconciliation and were readmitted to Communion. By the eleventh century there were very few remnants of this discipline of public penitence. In its place general confession and the imposition of ashes for the whole community had emerged. Lent now became a season of penitential acts for the whole church.

As early as the sixth century private penance had developed and general confession and absolution were aspects of the Eucharistic rite and the daily office. But by the Middle Ages a penitential system had emerged in which private individual confession to a priest as a representative of the congregation and forgiveness in the name of God and the community were offered. In time this practice became a yearly, trivial, and mechanical act. Worse, penance had become a means of buying forgiveness.

During the Reformation, an attempt was made to restore public penitence through the "fencing of the table" and church discipline. General confession, which had fallen out of practice, was given a new significance. Forgiveness was now freely and regularly available to all and private confessions diminished although their sacramental character was never denied. Later, individual confession and forgiveness was reinstituted in the form of Methodist Class Meetings and Anglican Oxford groups. Today, corporate confession at community liturgies, personal confession within small groups, and private confession to a priest all coexist in the Christian church. Correspondingly, a renewed understanding of congregational, corporate sin has surfaced and become the focus of general confession at daily offices and within the Eucharistic rites of the church.

The issue has never been, "will God forgive?" It has always been whether we will be forgiving to one another and accept forgiveness for ourselves. In the Lord's Prayer, we pray, "Forgive us our sins as we forgive those who sin against us," or as it might better be rendered, "Forgive us our sins that we might be enabled to forgive others their sins against us." God's forgiveness is an acknowledged fact, it only awaits our acceptance. Repentance, of course, is necessary since we cannot experience forgiveness until we realize we are in need of it. In this regard, it is important to note that repentance and forgiveness may or may not coincide with the sacramental action of reconciliation. What the sacramental action does is make real for us what is indeed already true.

It is important to acknowledge the importance of forgiving each other. It doesn't make sense to say only God can forgive and then recall Jesus' clear command that we have the responsibility to forgive. We cannot dodge our responsibility. If we humans hold back, the sinner is held back. We need to know not only God's forgiveness but the community's forgiveness as well. The record on God's forgiveness is clear. It is God's way to acquit the guilty. So much for justice. All God asks is that we be sorry and desirous of living otherwise. And even this latter requirement is only necessary because God does not want to force forgiveness upon us. Our contribution and penance does not win us forgiveness. Nothing is really necessary for God to forgive us.

Because every sin we commit affects the community, the com-

munity needs to be involved in reconciliation, in announcing forgiveness to sinners, aiding them to make new resolves, and helping
them to assimilate their new grace into their daily lives. In this regard, anyone may properly hear a confession and remind us of
God's grace. Indeed, in private confession the priest acts as a representative of the community and illumines for us our human need
to forgive each other.

For reconciliation to be meaningful it is important to differenti-
ate between three manifestations of sin. *Anxious guilt* results from
that sin which is best understood as our human existential condition, that sense of not being who we really are, that experience of
the soul's restlessness, that awareness of dis-ease, or being under
judgment. Traditionally this condition has been addressed by a
form of catechesis best described as spiritual guidance. Through the
daily examination of consciousness, meditation, and the devotional
reading of Scriptures and discernment exercises, we day by day confront anxious guilt and see our true condition. We have all been
justified and made whole by God's gracious act in Jesus Christ. We
celebrate our awareness of that fact in our baptism through an act
of faith. Thereby we enter upon that spiritual journey to fulfillment
traditionally described as sanctification. With the help of spiritual
exercises and guidance we actualize our human potential.

Neurotic guilt results from an unrealistic feeling of judgment. For
example, in neurotic sin, we feel guilt because of an action performed by our children or for an act in the distant past for which
we have been unable to accept God's forgiveness. Historically such
guilt has been addressed through pastoral counseling which aims to
free us from our neuroses.

Real guilt results from sin as an action identified by the community and ourselves as immoral. On occasion it is necessary for us to
admit that we have of our own free will acted in ways that have
denied our true human condition or caused others to be denied the
benefits of their true humanity. If we are sorrowful about this con-
crete, identifiable action or disposition of the heart and strongly
desire to live otherwise, the liturgical action of reconciliation is

proper and essential. Thus, we make our contrite confession and receive forgiveness in the name of God and the community through symbolic actions or rituals. We further identify that necessary penance which will aid us to live in grace. Penance is not a means of earning grace or making restitution for an act performed in the past—it is a set of catechetical actions which will aid us to live differently.

Reconciliation Catechesis
Certain fundamental problems face the average congregation in the use of reconciliation rites. The first is unfamiliarity; the second, a Protestant bias which makes personal confession to a clergyperson difficult. Most lay persons do not yet understand the difference between sin and sins, between sin and occasions for sin, between personal and corporate sin. A significant number of persons do not understand forgiveness and grace. Many more have an inadequate understanding of the nature and function of symbolic actions—rituals—and the representative, illuminary role of the priest or minister. Few understand the difference between real sin, neurotic sin, and cosmic sin. There are many who do not understand the function and purpose of the penitential rite in the daily office and the Eucharistic liturgy. Few have experienced communal liturgies of reconciliation. Almost none have ever made a personal, individual confession.

A significant catechetical program of experience and reflection with adults should be the first step. These programs should introduce adults to the various liturgical expressions of reconciliation. Further, the programs should provide basic theological information about sin and grace, liturgy and reconciliation. They also need to provide opportunities for reflection on experience and the place of forgiveness in our lives; that is, to rediscover the ongoing character of conversion and reconciliation. Related to this, we must encourage signs of conversion and reconciliation; namely, acts of charity and service, actions which require self-denial in the service of God and our neighbor.

Above all, we must urge people to forgive one another, thereby giving witness to the victory of love over sin. Only by participating in such actions and reflecting upon them can we come to understand that all Christian life is penitential. We must experience in community the acknowledgment of guilt and sorrow, and forgiveness and reconciliation or growth in grace before we can reflect on such experiences in the light of the Gospel faith. Catechesis for reconciliation will require an experiential (action-reflection) catechesis first for adults and then through adults for children.

Catechesis and Reconciliation
Communal liturgies of reconciliation for families, especially during Advent and Lent, should be reintroduced. We cannot overlook the catechetical value of these neglected communal rites of penance on special occasions, as well as special ceremonials such as the Stations or Way of the Cross which are being reintroduced into Protestant spirituality. Catechesis within these rites can take place through Scripture and homily.

Further, catechesis for parents must enable them to treat their children at home and church in ways that make possible the children's awareness of their true humanity as loveable, trustable, capable persons of worth. Parents also need help in learning how to use times of family crisis and estranged interpersonal relations to express forgiveness and reconciliation, to help children understand the meaning of the sad sights they see in the news reports and the negative experiences they have with their peers. We also need to encourage parents to have their children join them in acts of love and service and to reflect upon such actions as signs of our redeemed life in Christ.

Beginning with adolescence, we must help persons to understand that the rite of reconciliation is not simply a formal ceremony in which we experience forgiveness; it is a dialogue in faith between two of God's believing people. People need to be helped to identify sins to be confessed, to express their sin, and to reflect upon acts of penance, i.e. catechetical aids to help them live a more Christian life.

Catechesis Within the Rite of Reconciliation

The period of dialogue within the confessional is to serve a cate-chetical function and needs to become a major aspect of this im-portant ritual. Within the rite of reconciliation for a penitent, there are directions which read, "Here the priest may offer counsel, di-rection, and comfort." Clergy and laity must learn to engage in this conversation, offer and receive pastoral counseling or spiritual di-rection as needed, and frame those "spiritual exercises" of penance which will aid the reconciled person to live out the grace he or she has been offered and accepted.

Penitential Rubrics

The prayer of confession in the daily office and the Eucharistic rite is essential during Advent and Lent, optional during ordinary times, and inappropriate during Christmastide and Eastertide. While a penitential focus is essential during Advent and Lent, the rest of the year should focus on our nature as a redeemed commu-nity. For too long we have emphasized our human condition as "miserable worms" or as sinners whose potential is extremely lim-ited. While we cannot and ought not ignore our sin, we also need to focus on our redeemed state as a people. This is the proper van-tage point for viewing our sin. We experience through our litur-gies our new, redeemed condition with its potential for goodness and love.

The prayer of confession can rightly come at either the beginning of the service, prior to the lessons, or following the prayers of the people. In many psychological ways, the latter position appears more appropriate, especially since it is followed by the kiss of peace in which the community expresses reconciliation through a con-crete symbolic act. In any case, it is important to maintain the pe-riod of silence following the call to confession so that persons may reflect on their individual and corporate life and thereby bring their confessions into corporate expression. In that regard, we want to take a strong stand against the writing of original prayers of con-fession to be used by the congregation, unless there are community awareness of and agreement on particular sins which these prayers can express and skillful use of corporate prayer language. Writing original prayers of confession too often degenerates into the presentation of the pastor's hidden agenda. This is not good catechesis; the prayer of confession is not the place to educate persons about what they might confess.

Corporate services of penitence and reconciliation should be provided during the church year or when the life experience of the community necessitates such corporate actions. We must be sensitive to such moments and provide for their communal celebration, particularly during penitential seasons such as Lent, beginning with the imposition of ashes on Ash Wednesday and continuing through the Good Friday service.

Established times should be provided to encourage persons to make personal confessions—especially during those seasons when the corporate prayers of confession are omitted from the Sunday liturgy. During the early adolescent years, we must stress the importance of persons, making their first confession and must prepare youth for this event. While in some communions a first confession has been traditional for young children, there are good reasons developmentally to save the rite until persons have acquired mature consciences and can make a confession that has real meaning for them.

· 14 ·

Ministration to the Sick

While health is a major concern of contemporary people, our theoretically enlightened era has neglected and discouraged sacramental and devotional practices of healing. While such practices have never died out in the Christian world, they have been restricted to places such as Lourdes and to groups such as the Pentecostals and Christian Scientists. In place of religion and the priest, medical science and the physician have assumed the sole role in human health. Of course, much of this is slowly changing. In recent years medicine has discovered that illness can have causes that are not physical. Physicians have also realized that the human being cannot be treated as only a physical being, but must be treated as a whole functioning social organism which includes that person's faith and religious life. Still, the average lay person or clergyperson has limited interest in or experience of physical, emotional, or spiritual healing through religious means. Nevertheless, most religious communities have new rituals for ministration to the sick and communal healing liturgies.

But questions remain. What is the place of healing in the church? How does God act in human life? What function does prayer play in our human experience? The church today is divided over the answers to these questions.

Most Christian churches seem to believe that they have nothing to do with healing the sick. They do not feel that the church's symbolic actions—rituals—have any direct effect on human health. Few clergy or hospital chaplains feel comfortable with spiritual healing. Indeed, many hospital chaplains assume the dress, the white coats, of physicians and become identified with the professional medical staff.

Oddly enough this is antithetical to historical Christian faith. The change came slowly, but it began in the tenth century when the service of unction (anointing) for healing became *extreme unction* for the dying. Thus the sacrament for the healing of the human being in this world became the sacrament for the healing (saving) of the human being in the next world. Healing in the church shifted to shrines and relics, both of which the Reformation cast aside. In place of Christian sacramental healing, three alternative views emerged and were accepted by the church. One view accepted a totally materialistic conception of the human being and therefore asserted that religious acts were superfluous because the human body can only be cared for by physical or medical means. A *second view* affirmed that God was responsible for sickness. While religious acts will not cure us, only medical science can do that, the minister's task is to save a person's soul, since God sent the illness so that persons might be converted and/or grow in faith. A *third* asserted that Jesus and the church did indeed have a healing ministry, but that God in time gave us the gift of medical science, so that the accounts of religious healing in the New Testament and the early church, while surely accurate, are no longer possible. In any case, Christian healing through sacramental acts was no longer taken seriously.

Two possibilities for understanding reality exist. The first assumes a closed rational physical world of sense experience. In this view there is no reality apart from the known world of sense experience and reason, and it is incongruous that we might be influenced by any reality independent of the physical world. Consistent with this understanding, there is no responsive or intuitional mode of consciousness, no emotional or nonrational aspect to human experience. Instead there is only an active or intellectual mode of consciousness. In this view faith becomes rational, logical. Belief and revelation become a theological dogmatic system to be accepted for salvation. Without any place for a spiritual (non-material) reality, sacramental healing is a logical absurdity. By the close of the Middle Ages this enlightenment view of reality dominated Christian thought. It persists into the present.

Still another, more traditional view is possible. This viewpoint contends that reality is composed of two dimensions: there are *both* a real physical world and a real nonphysical world, *both* an active intellectual mode of consciousness and a responsive intuitive mode of consciousness. Faith, in this view, becomes that perceptual field necessary for salvation and revelation, a relational experience of God and the vocational daily individual and corporate life in both the material and nonmaterial dimension of reality. In this case, sacramental healing becomes one of the direct ways in which the spiritual and material worlds interact.

Today it is the scientific community that has begun to question rational materialism and its closed naturalistic system. Once again the significance of the traditional Christian understanding of reality has resurfaced. Equipped with a new understanding of the unconscious, a new understanding of experience and our place in the universe has emerged. The human being is the bridge between the objective physical dimension of reality and the subjective, psychic or spiritual dimension.

Human life must develop and integrate the intellectual and intuitional modes of consciousness. Knowledge comes to us through experimental, non-verbal, irrational means and is then reflected upon and rationally described. Really, the world has both spiritual, non-material dimensions and physical, material dimensions. Thus the religious undertaking and the religious object are not only potentially meaningful, they are necessary if we are to be whole, healthy persons. Once again, a world view is possible for people today that not only has a new appreciation of the vital experience of Christian revelation, but also supports an understanding of Christian sacramental healing.

Jesus healed with a word and a touch. There are, therefore, three parts to the rite of ministration to the sick. The *first* is a ministry of the word. The *second* is the laying on of hands and anointing. The Scriptures are a call to faith, to that perception necessary if healing is to be accepted and recognized. The laying on of hands and anointing are historical, symbolic acts claiming the person for God's kingdom and rule. This part provides a blessing in the form of the exchange of energy or the power of God's spirit. Holy Communion, the *third* part, celebrates the presence of Christ in our lives, transforming our brokenness and incompleteness into salvation and wholeness.

Catechesis and Ministration to the Sick

It will be impossible for persons to participate meaningfully in a ministry of healing without an adequate intellectual explanation and theological framework from which to understand what can and does occur in sacramental healing. Without this understanding, emotionalism and magic will prevail. We must help persons acquire a belief in a spiritual or nonmaterial reality and an understanding of the responsive intuitive mode of consciousness. A theology of the Spirit needs to be developed and reflected upon so that persons can come to see that there is no conflict between the practice of medical healing and the legitimate, sacramental healing ministry of the church.

The church must provide a place where there can be frank and honest discussion of the issues and questions related to spiritual healing, and particular interpretations of sickness should be addressed. The theory that God sends illness as a punishment for disobedience should be questioned. Such a view makes God a tyrant rather than a loving parent. This must be rejected. Still, it would be foolish to rule out this element entirely—we can will ourselves to be sick. Guilt can cause illness, and forgiveness can heal the spirit and hence the body. The theory that sickness is either punishment or training to endure the long hard pilgrimage of life must also be reflected upon. This view distorts an understanding of God as loving and righteous; it must be rejected.

Further, the theory that sickness is a mark of Satan's rule over the world or the assertion that the existence of sickness is an unresolved enigma in human life, a power hostile to us and often stronger than we are, must be explored. In this case, the Christian Gospel proclaims the power of God to set things right. This may mean physical healing or emotional healing or the power to live purposefully and meaningfully with sickness. What is important is that we always affirm and advocate the treatment of physical and emotional disease by the best methods which modern science affords. Faith in the Christian mystery establishes an attitude of confidence in the face of sickness, a confidence which can be part of the cure. Healing may come by either or both medical science or prayer and the sacramental actions of the church.

Persons need experiences of a caring community growing in love and experience of God. The focus of catechesis will be on helping persons develop, in community, a vital relationship with the Spirit. Unless spiritual life as well as spiritual understandings are nurtured, rites of ministration to the sick will be limited.

Persons should be introduced to the church's historical and contemporary individual and communal healing rites. Before these healing services can become a vital aspect of personal and church life, persons should be exposed to them and helped to understand what is said and done within them.

It is important for persons to understand that healing is related to physical, emotional, or spiritual sickness. Most people think of healing only in terms of physical disease. A person can participate in a sacramental act of healing for a troubled spirit, for sick emotions such as despair, depression, and the like, and for ill bodies. We must be aware that we are whole persons in whom every aspect of our humanity influences every other. Sick bodies can cause us to suffer emotionally. Emotional illness can affect our bodies. Healing of one part of us will influence the rest of us. We also need to understand that while the rite of reconciliation can minister to those who cause hurt, the rite of healing can minister to those who have been hurt.

Catechesis Within the Ministration to the Sick
Within the rites of the church for healing is the Ministry of the Word, composed of readings from the Holy Scripture with the op-

portunity for a homily or interpretive comment. It is important that we not ignore this element or neglect the necessary role that catechesis can play to help a person prepare for faithful participation in the laying on of hands, prayers, anointing, and Holy Communion.

Catechesis for the Ministration to the Sick
Until the church's rites of sacramental healing become commonplace, we will need to alert persons both to the possibilities of celebrating them and what it might mean for these persons if they participate in them.

Further, with these rites there is an opportunity for the reconciliation of a penitent. In preparation for the rite, the person can be helped to examine his or her conscience so that it can be determined if this special confession will be relevant. Personal catechesis will be necessary for this decision.

Rubrics for Ministration to the Sick
Our rites with the sick focus first on the ministry of the Word—because the sick ought to hear their sickness interpreted and set in the context of the Gospel. We are assuming that the liturgy with the sick be used in an individual or small group setting. The tone should be informal, warm, and compassionate. On some occasions, when the person and the person's sickness have an especially "public" character, appropriate scripture texts are: II Corinthians 1:3-5 and Luke 17:11-19. After scripture and some brief, informal reflection upon or response to the scripture, either private or general confession may be made. Hebrews 12:1-2, Psalm 103, and Matthew 9:2-8 are among the appropriate texts for this portion of the rite.

The essential, symbolic activity at the time of illness is the laying on of hands with anointing. A blessing should be said over the oil. Oil is used as a tangible, visible means of conveying our care and God's grace. Historically, oil was used for cleansing and medicinal purposes. The sign of the cross may be made upon the person's forehead. Hands and feet may also be anointed. This action should be done with tenderness and care.

The third and final part of the ministration to the sick is the celebration of the Eucharist. This should be done as briefly and informally as possible, using a bedside table. Avoid the use of miniature, doll-sized vessels which tend to trivialize the sacrament. It is possible to simply use vessels which are in the home or hospital for this purpose. When communion elements are brought directly from a Eucharistic service at the church to the sick person for communion, this emphasizes the corporate, communal nature of the sacrament and the continuing support of the Christian fellowship in time of sickness.

·15·

Ministration at the Time of Death and Burial of the Dead

The seasons of our lives do not endure forever. The Christian life cycle begins at baptism. It ends in death. The church has always seen a foreshadowing of our end in our beginning. Baptism, as we noted in chapter 1, has always been compared to death. It is our womb and also our tomb. In our baptism we start getting ready for death, dying to all that enslaves us, dying to our old selves, dying so that we may be reborn.

So Luther could speak of baptism as dress rehearsal for death. It is our first experience of letting go, of casting ourselves upon the mercy of the everlasting arms, of giving up hope in ourselves so that we may hope only in God. Every day you must die, Luther observed, so that every day God can cause you to be born to the new creation he is making of you. When they asked Luther if he feared death, he could say, "No, because I have already died a hundred deaths, beginning in my baptism, and I cannot fear what I have already done."

The Christian's hope at death is the same hope which sustains the Christian throughout life: that the God who has claimed us, and loved us, and grasped us in life will continue to claim us, and love us, and grasp us in death.

In a death-denying and death-avoiding society, the church is able to boldly and confidently face that which the world spends most of its time running away from. The church is able to do this, not because of our hope for eternal life, but because of our bold and confident faith in the eternal love of God. We expect death from the beginning. It does not come as a surprise to us. It is that which we spend our lives preparing for, participating in. As Augustine said in one of his sermons:

> As when medical men examine an illness, and ascertain that it is fatal, they make this pronouncement, "He will die, he will not get over this," so from the moment of a man's birth, it may be said, "He will not get over this."
>
>   Sermon 47, 3; NPNF VI:412

We are able to have a peculiar realism about death because we have a peculiar hope in God.

The Church's Past Dealings with Death

As with a number of the church's pastoral offices, we have little information on early Christian burial practices. Funerals, or anything like funerals, are not mentioned in the New Testament. Descriptions of Christian burial in the third century indicate some continuation of pagan burial customs: a last meal for the dead, washing and clothing of the body, a procession to the grave, a funeral oration, and subsequent commemoration of the dead on specified occasions. Early Christians appear to have made some notable changes in these inherited pagan customs: the Eucharist was often celebrated at the grave, the kiss of peace was given to the corpse before burial, victorious white garments, songs and psalms of praise were substituted for the customary pagan black vestments and mournful dirges.

Death was often referred to by early Christians as a "heavenly birthday," signifying that a Christian dies in order to be born into eternity. The white vestments, songs of praise, and joy of these funeral celebrations must have been quite a contrast to the somber pagan practices. The dead Christian who had kept the faith was treated as a victor, one who had fought a good fight and was now borne forth triumphantly into the eternal presence of God.

During the Middle Ages, Christian funeral practices moved from victory to fear. The medieval church's preoccupation with thoughts of hell, purgatory, and judgment colored the liturgical response to death. Death was seen, not as a step on the way to triumph, but as the final accounting, a prelude to last judgment. As was typical of the medieval church's dealings with baptism, the Eucharist, and many of the pastoral offices, medieval funeral practices were concerned with an individual's sin, absolution, and the status of the person's soul.

The churches of the Reformation, while protesting against the mournful character of medieval funerals, the medieval preoccupation with the status of the dead person's soul and, as Luther called it, "Hocus-pocus on behalf of the dead," failed to restore a strong focus on hope and comfort. Perhaps because of their disagreement with medieval funeral practices, few of the Reformers constructed new funerals. Luther stressed the importance of hymns of hope and comfort and the preached word at funerals but left no burial rite. The Reformed churches likewise stressed funeral sermons but were suspicious of all funeral liturgies and symbolic actions. Reformed burial services tended to be primarily scripture and sermon (which often degenerated into a eulogy extolling the alleged virtues or a censure condemning the alleged vices of the deceased). Anglicans had a bit more developed funeral and burial liturgy but, like other churches of the Reformation, tended to bury people with a minimum of ritual and no congregational participation.

Funeral practices in the church of our own era have inherited many of the shortcomings of our past dealings with death. Most of our funerals have been somber, mournful, weak on solid Christian affirmations, or any sense of corporate participation by the faithful. Unfortunately, the result has been that, in modern times, our funerals are often more pagan than Christian. Because our liturgies have said so little, we moderns have inevitably said too much, claimed to know too much, and speculated too idly on the mystery of death. The result has been that the church's valid ministry at the time of death has often been obscured by all sorts of non-Christian accretions; the church's good news was covered by flowers, eulogies, poetry, and garish extravagance.

The new funeral liturgies attempt to restore some positive elements of the early church's dealing with death. While scripture is prominent in these new services, there are more opportunities for sacramental, congregational participation as the whole people of God join in affirming what we believe at the time of death and in ministering to our bereft brothers and sisters. These new rites therefore recognize that the focus of the Christian ministry at time of death is twofold: to proclaim and show God's love at the time of death; and to commend the deceased to God's grace.

First, the Christian funeral provides the church a wonderful opportunity to proclaim and show forth the faith which we hold and which holds us in time of death. Our funeral rites are services of worship—not mere utilitarian occasions to dispose of a body nor simply an opportunity to care for a grieving individual. As in any service of Christian worship, the primary focus of our liturgical response to death should be upon God. As in life, God's love and grace are our hope in death—not our good lives or our good deeds.

Throughout the various formal and informal rituals which surround death, the church should speak, in word and sacrament, to our hope. Our hope is based, not on who we are or what we have done, but upon our lifelong, daily experience of what God has done. The resurrection is the core of our theological witness at death. We proclaim that, just as God raised Jesus on the third day, so we too participate in that joyous gift.

And it is a gift. We do not believe in the noble pagan myth of the immortality of the soul. Immortality is not a human characteristic, not something which is part of human nature. As the Psalmist says, "Our days are like grass, they flourish in the morning, by evening they have withered." Eternal life is not some human achievement or innate human possession. It is a gift, a surprising, graceful gift of an eternal God who loves us every day of our lives, loves us in life, and then loves us in death so that he may love us forever.

Thus, resurrection is a mighty act of God, a gift, the last re-creating which God does in us so that we may be fit to bear his image within us forever. At the time of death, we have no other witness, no other comfort than this.

Ministration at the Time of Death

When death is imminent, when the last breath of life is near, when loved ones realize that their beloved is close to death, the church begins its ministrations. Actually, the church should be involved, if circumstances permit, long before the moment of death, in the rituals for the sick (Chapter 14) as well as the church's continuous, lifelong effort to prepare its people for death.

EXAMPLE:

The liturgy of Ministration at the time of Death in the *Book of Common Prayer* is intended to minister to all those close to the dying when death is imminent. When possible, this is an extremely important liturgy for it begins a necessary period of transition. When an unexpected death occurs, some sort of liturgy such as the laying of a headstone is necessary to put closure on the transition from life to death among the community.

Ideally, the funeral should be the culminating event in a process of corporate care of the mourners. The caring congregation usually has a whole series of formal and informal rituals which happen automatically at the time of death. Among the historical practices which occur before the actual burial service is the *vigil*. A vigil occurs sometime before the funeral itself, at the home or in the church. It should be a time for family and friends to gather and begin to gather their thoughts and feelings about the death. Suitable psalms, lessons, and prayers (such as those within the burial rite itself) may be used. The setting, form, and length of the rite should be determined by local tradition and other circumstances.

The actual *burial service* usually consists of the following elements: prayers, hymns and anthems, psalms, scripture lessons, sermon, prayers, and Eucharist. The church is the most appropriate place for this service. The body should be present, a visible, tangible sign of the death which has occurred. This is a time for remembrance, proclamation, and prayer.

Finally, there is the *committal,* the committal of the deceased to the earth or wherever the body's final resting place shall be, and the committal of our beloved brother or sister to the love and grace of God. The committal is a visible, symbolic statement of both the reality of this death, the finality of it, and also the hope inherent in giving this person back to the God who gave the person to us.

Generally speaking, the burial of the dead is one of the most free-form of the church's services. Most service books give the pastor and congregation wide latitude in supplementing the service, adapting it, and modifying it to suit the cultural context of the congregation, local customs, or the specific circumstances of death. This means that, in the ministration at time of death and burial of the dead, we are faced with fewer liturgical norms and specific guides than in many of the church's other services.

This freedom and adaptability of most liturgies for death and burial relate to the first liturgical norm for the funeral. *The service of Christian burial serves, first, to comfort the bereaved.* When we gather as a church at a funeral, we are not gathering to focus on death and resurrection in general, but upon a specific death of a specific person whom we have known and loved. Some of us, in reacting against older funerals which sometimes degenerated into long eulogies and inappropriate celebrations of the alleged vices or virtues of the deceased, have turned our funerals into impersonal, generalized, detached rituals which are careful to make no reference to the person who has died, or to the loved ones who are going through an acute crisis of grief. This is theologically questionable and pastorally insensitive. We not only gather to proclaim the church's word at death to the whole church, but to proclaim a specific, even personal word to those in our midst who now go through a specific crisis in life. We name and claim a specific brother or sister in Christ who has died, and is now to be named among the saints.

This also means that we need to allow for some flexibility in our liturgical response to death. The family may have various requests for the content of the service. The liturgical planners and leaders of the church must struggle to provide guidelines for what is generally appropriate or inappropriate for a Christian funeral without restricting the service of death and burial to the point that the grieving family and friends are unable to do what they need to do in order to move through this crisis.

Psychologists remind us that grief requires work, "grief work," which is often painful but absolutely necessary. People respond to death in different ways which are deeply expressive of a person's deepest feelings and beliefs. We must take care not to label or judge these responses or unduly restrict a person's need to act out the myriad of thoughts and feelings which the death of a loved one occasions. We may not "grieve as those who have no hope," as Paul says, but we still grieve. The church's liturgical response to death should give people the space and freedom to grieve.

At the same time, ministration to the grieving family and friends, acknowledgment of and response to the needs and wishes of the family and friends are not our only concerns. The second purpose of a Christian service of death and burial, the second norm under which we must plan and evaluate our liturgies of death and burial is that *services of death and burial are worship services of the church.*

As we said at the beginning of this book, we gather, at any service of worship, not simply to do things for people, even to do very good things for people. We gather to be with God. Death offers the church a wonderful opportunity to be with its God in one of life's most difficult and beautiful moments. This tells us that when we evaluate our liturgical response to death, we can use the same standards of evaluation which apply to any of the church's corporate services of worship: Is the service scriptural? Does it have ample opportunity for corporate, active, congregational involvement? Does it lift up the self-giving of God through the sacraments? Does it faithfully articulate the church's teaching and witness at this occasion in the life cycle? Does it relate this experience to the current season of the church's year? No doubt you will think of others.

When judged by standards for a full, theologically and biblically responsible service of worship, many of our traditional funerals are woefully inadequate. Sometimes, in a misguided effort to be "pastoral," caring for the needs and wishes of a grieving family, the church has offered the family false consolation, false hope which was not ours to offer, or else we have smothered the church's true witness and legitimate word in a mass of pagan accretions, flowers, extravagance, pomp, and sentiment. At the funeral, we must speak the truth in love, but we must examine ourselves to be sure that we really do speak the truth.

With these two, sometimes contradictory, sometimes difficult to balance, norms for the service of death and burial in mind, let us look at educational strategies for these services.

Catechesis for Time of Death and Burial of the Dead

Because of the great trauma and dislocation which the death of a loved one usually causes in persons, the time of death is obviously not the best time to prepare people for participation in our liturgies for the bereaved. Preparation for participating in the ministration at time of death and burial should be an ongoing, constant pastoral concern of the community.

There is no Christian community that is not constantly dealing with death. It may not be dealing with a specific occasion of death, but death is always a concern. At any given moment in the community's life together, while we may not be dealing with a specific, current, acute crisis of grief, we are dealing with grief. There are those who are preparing for *future grief,* seeking clues, guidelines, meanings, and rituals which will be helpful at the time of some future bereavement. There are also people who are dealing with *past grief,* seeking clues, guidelines, meanings, and rituals which will be helpful in coping with past grief.

This communal, ongoing nature of "grief work" reminds us that the pastoral focus of the funeral and our pre- and post-burial activities is not only upon a specific grieving family which is going through an immediate crisis of grief. We are also focusing on past and future "grief work" of the entire congregation.

Who is a funeral for? It is for *all of us.* The whole church. Therefore, as Christian educators prepare Christians for participation in the church's ministration at the time of death, as we plan our liturgies which relate to death, let us remember that we are planning for and educating the whole church. We are called to minister first to a specific grieving family, but not only to this family. We are ministering to the whole family of God. In the liturgy, we want to lift up the memories, affirmations, and thoughts of a specific grieving family, but not only of this family. We lift up the memory, affirmation, and testimony of the church.

Our educational strategies for our liturgical response to death must continue this twofold focus of the church at the time of death. We want to enable people to do the very private, personal, heartfelt things they may need to do when a loved one dies. But we also want to enable the whole church to do what it needs to do at the time of death.

We can help prepare individuals for participation in our ministrations of death by helping them focus upon death before death occurs. Because there is often much confusion and misinformation in this matter, pastors would be wise to periodically preach about death. In sermons, the preacher can articulate the Christian belief about death and resurrection. The pastor may wish to contrast the pagan belief in the immortality of the soul with the Christian affirmation of the resurrection of the body. At such times, the pastor may wish to remind the congregation that he or she is the true "funeral director," the first to be called at time of death, the one to be consulted in all funeral arrangements, the best resource person in the congregation for planning and thinking about funerals. In preaching and teaching about death, the pastor conveys to the congregation a sense that Christians can dare to speak about that which most of our world spends most of its life seeking to avoid. We need not deny death, because we have something to say in the face of the final enemy.

Some congregations have found it helpful to keep a "funeral file," in which a printed form is given to each member of the congregation to fill out regarding specific requests or plans for his or her funeral. This can be a good means of enabling people to think about their death and can also be a kind and loving thing for people to do for their loved ones. Knowing that "he wanted it this way" can relieve a family of many difficult decisions at the time of death.

A congregational statement about death along with guidelines for services of death and burial are essential work for a worship committee. Such guidelines help to educate everyone about appropriate responses, options, and rites of death and burial.

Funerals should be held, if at all possible, when the majority of the congregation can be present. The presence and participation of the congregation is not only of great help and comfort to a grieving family but also a means of helping the congregation prepare for future grief experiences and to deal with past grief, as we mentioned earlier. Never forget that, as with other services of worship, every time we participate in this worship, we are learning through the liturgy.

As with any rite of passage, our rituals for death and burial can be divided into three parts: separation, transition, and incorporation. Failure to adequately involve the community and the grieving persons in any one part of the passage process can defeat the movement of grieving persons through the process.

It would be helpful for the congregation or its liturgy committee to evaluate its rituals related to death, using the rite of passage model. This can be done by simply listing all of the activities which are done at time of death. One congregation's analysis looked like this:

	Informal Rituals (unwritten)	**Formal Rituals** (written)
• SEPARATION Grieving persons separated from rest of community so they may be the focus of community care.	Body taken to funeral home. Family's daily routine stops. Flowers placed on front door.	Altar Guild prepares for funeral.
• TRANSITION Betwixt and between. Period for education, reflection, preparation for new life status.	Food brought in by congregation for the family and friends. Wake or vigil. Arrangements and planning for the service of death and burial. Obituary appears in newspapers. Visits by family and friends. Viewing the body at the funeral home.	Vigil service at home. Service of death at the church. Burial service at cemetery.
• INCORPORA-TION Grieving family integrated back into community.	Pastor makes follow-up visits to the home. Friends continue to check on family. Financial affairs are set in order.	Prayers said for the deceased and the bereaved at church service on the following Sunday.

The actual service of death and burial recapitulates, encapsulates the full process of separation, transition, and incorporation. Sometimes, whether the formal, public ritual of corporate worship "works" for the community and the grieving family is dependent upon whether all the informal, pre-service rituals have been carried out. What we do before and after funerals is therefore of great importance.

EXAMPLE:

When the liturgy of Ministration at the Time of Death is celebrated with dying persons and those closest to them; for example, with a terminal cancer patient or in final phases of muscular dystrophy, heart conditions, etc.—personal catechesis with the dying to prepare them for death and address this concern and question as well as small group catechesis for the family can be extremely helpful. Our tendency is to hide from death. Every congregation at any one time has a number of persons whose illness is terminal. Catechesis with their families, perhaps led by those who have witnessed similar deaths, would be extremely important.

Rubrics for the Service of Death and Burial

The vigil has been a neglected part of our liturgical response to death in many churches. This is unfortunate since this can be a very personal, important time of preparation for the funeral. The vigil can take place the evening before the funeral, in the home or in the church. Prayers, scripture, and psalms and songs may be used. Sometimes, if the family has specific requests related to the funeral services, such as the deceased person's favorite song or poem or some special reading they would like to hear, the vigil may be a more appropriate time to do this rather than the more public service of corporate worship which the funeral itself should be. The vigil can become a wonderful time to reminisce, tell funny stories about our memories of the life of the person who has died, and, in general, celebrate the life of the one whom we have known and loved.

The planning and leadership of the service of death and burial assumes that much has occurred before this service takes place. The presence and participation of the congregation will be encouraged through the use of congregational response such as hymns, responsive prayers, creeds, and other acts of corporate worship. So far as possible, the service ought to closely resemble, in its form and tone, a typical Sunday service. This helps to reinforce the idea that the funeral is a service of worship, not some unusual, detached experience which has a focus other than that of usual Christian worship.

While we want this service to be an adequate statement of the church's historical witness at the time of death, we also want the service to be personal to some extent. United Methodists, in their new Service of Death and Resurrection, suggest that, after the sermon, members of the congregation may wish to offer brief statements of thanksgiving for the life of the deceased.

Most of us need to give closer attention to the role of symbol and gesture in our services of death and burial. We know that, during the crisis of grief, our feelings and actions are usually more expressive of our needs than words. We are talking about "grief *work*" which must be *done,* not simply discussed. And yet, many of our inherited funeral liturgies are almost exclusively verbal, without symbol or gesture. Anyone who has gone through grief can testify that during the crisis of death one loving hand upon the shoulder can mean more than a dozen sermons on death.

We also need to examine the role of the symbolic within our services. Many older funeral customs which have been purged from our formal and informal rituals for funerals need to be examined again in the light of what we know about the needs of people at the time of grief. Preparation of the body by friends, construction of a coffin, the making of a shroud, pallbearers who *really* carry a coffin in and out of a church (rather than walk behind the coffin as the funeral director rolls it in on a cart), the use of a pall, the casting of dirt on the coffin after the commitment, the actual covering of the coffin with dirt can all be visible, tangible, therapeutic ways of helping people act out their needs related to death.

Thus the life cycle ends, borne from the womb to the tomb through the gift of the liturgy, sustained by God's presence, experienced among God's people and their rites, nurtured by the self-giving of God through the sacraments. All this our God does for us through his grace, nurturing us, disciplining us, lovingly forming his image in us in this life, here, today, with only one good purpose in mind—so that he may love us in the life to come, forever.

In the words of the anthem at the committal in the rite for the burial of the dead, *Book of Common Prayer:*

> Everyone the Father gives to me will come to me; I will never turn away anyone who believes in me.
>
> He who raised Jesus Christ from the dead will also give new life to our mortal bodies through the indwelling Spirit.
>
> My heart, therefore, is glad, and my spirit rejoices; my body also shall rest in hope.
>
> You will show me the path of life; in your presence there is fullness of joy, and in your right hand are pleasures forever-more.

And so we remember that when our life within this church on earth comes to a close, our eternal life among the heavenly chorus begins. Together may we always look to God in hope for the actualization of salvation and God's rule on earth. And may those of us who remain never forget our baptismal covenant to continue in the apostles' teaching and fellowship, in the breaking of bread, and in prayer; to persevere in resisting evil and whenever we fall into sin, repent and return to the Lord; to proclaim by word as example the Good News of God in Christ; to seek to serve Christ in all persons; loving our neighbor as ourselves; and to strive for justice and peace among all people, respecting the dignity of every human being. And may we also pray that those who are now living the resurrected life may help us to be faithful in our liturgical and catechetical life during our pilgrimage toward sanctification in community.

Notes

1. John H. Westerhoff, III in Gwen Kennedy Neville and John H. Westerhoff, III, *Learning Through Liturgy* (New York: Seabury Press, 1978), p. 91.
2. *ibid.*
3. William H. Willimon, *Worship As Pastoral Care* (Nashville: Abingdon Press, 1979), p. 12.
4. *ibid.,* p. 48.
5. William H. Willimon, *Word, Water, Wine, and Bread* (Valley Forge, Pa.: Judson Press, 1980), p. 7.
6. *ibid.,* p. 6.
7. *Remember Who You Are: Baptism and the Christian Life* (Nashville: Abingdon Press, 1980) by William H. Willimon (with educational guide by John H. Westerhoff, III). Could be a helpful resource for individuals and parishes wishing to explore contemporary meanings and issues of baptism.
8. *Saying Yes to Marriage* (Valley Forge, Pa.: Judson Press, 1979) by William H. Willimon. Could provide pastors and worship or religious education committees essential biblical and theological background on Christian marriage.